Help Lord, I'm Afraid!

Help Lord, I'm Afraid!

By Laura Irby

DgrChristianBooks.com

Unless otherwise indicated, all Scripture quotations are taken from the New International Version of the Bible.

Copyright @ 2009

Help Lord, I'm Afraid! - by Laura Irby

ISBN 978-0-9796077-6-9
ISBN 0-9796077-6-0
Library of Congress Control Number:

Edited and contributions by:

Joan

Published By:
DGR Christian Books
DGRChristianbooks.com

Help Lord, I'm Afraid!

From fearful fallacy (our wrong thinking), to a fearless fortress (a strong fortified place that builds defenses)-God! .... a 39 day Voyage through the Old Testament (From Genesis –Malachi)

The only thing we have to fear is not a thing: As believers we are called to fear The Fearless One

'Laura Irby'

This book is dedicated to my mother whose courage to raise her children by herself-not receiving child support because her ex-husband was in prison-working three jobs to give her family a good Christmas-has made me the woman I am today. You are a woman who became free to fly from your fears and encouraged me to do the same-to Soar~! Thanks mom

Psalm 56: 3 "When I am afraid, I will trust in you."

Honorable Mention

I love you David. You are a man who truly lives life without fear. You have been an example of a man who trusts in God. Thank you for teaching me what it means to _really_ trust in God and to live without fear. Thank you for not allowing fear in our marriage. Thank you for encouraging me to write even when I wanted to give up. Thank you for pushing me to get this to the publisher.

To Dad- God knew who my parents would be. He had a purpose and a plan. God reconciled us in His time. Without 'our story' this book may not have been written. The Living Water has brought you and I on an amazing voyage that has taught me how to overcome fear and that God's strength is made perfect in weakness.

Thank you Joan for editing this book.

Thanks to our brother in the Lord Richard who lived with us in the process of finishing up this book and saw first hand our struggles and attacks from the evil one. Thank you for praying for this book, and our marriage, to come to completion.

Take a Voyage with the "Fearless Fortress"

Let Him lead you from one place to another in your life until all fear is out of your life completely! God is fearless-and He is our mighty fortress.

Change your fearful fallacy (wrong thinking)

Believe!

He thinks you're beautiful, always.

Today, August 11, 2009, I asked God how you were doing.

What was God's answer?

God said, "My child is beautiful today."

This is a true story. I asked a girl at work how her newborn daughter was doing. She got all choked up and said, "She is beautiful."

It was as though the new mother didn't even hear that I asked her _how_ the baby was doing. I didn't ask her what the baby looked like.

However, to this mom her new daughter is so beautiful to her in her heart. The bible says, "Out of the abundance of the heart the mouth speaks."

Whenever the mother thinks about her daughter she simply thinks, "My daughter is beautiful."

I got choked up thinking about the fact that this is how God sees all of His children. It is not based on what we do or don't do. Our beauty in Him is based solely because He created us.

I then heard the still small voice of God say to me, "Write this in your book. Tell all *my children* that I think they are beautiful."

His love for us is eternal. He forgives your sins as far as the East is from the West. He thinks you're beautiful no matter what!

To Him we are always beautiful.

Introduction

The reason why I call this book a Voyage instead of a journey is because of the definition.

The word Voyage in Webster's means:

A trip or a journey, especially by water, from one place to another.

One of God's names is the Living Water, and the Living Water takes us on an amazing journey from Genesis to Malachi and tells us to have no fear for HE is alive!

Come take this Voyage with me from Genesis-Malachi and allow the Living Water, the fearless fortress to free you from all your fears!

The definition of *fear* in Webster's Dictionary for Students is this: A strong unpleasant feeling caused by being aware of danger or expecting something bad to happen.

The definition of *fearless* (which is our goal) in Webster's Dictionary for Students is this: FREE FROM FEAR~!

The definition of fallacy is: Wrong or faulty thinking.

The definition of fortress is: A fortified place.

The word fortified is: To make strong, (to build defenses.)

This leads me to believe that it is possible to be free from fear. Our fear is based on our faulty thinking.
We can be led to a fearless fortress in our life. God is the ultimate fearless fortress.

God wants all His children to be fearless because He is the One who is strong and defends us. Scripture tells us that He is our fortress!

 The opposite of fear is Trust. If you or I are trusting in God Almighty for our provision and not our job or our abilities or skills or talents then we can be free from fear. If we trust in our own strength for our provision then we are not trusting in God our creator to be our Jehovah Jireh. One of God's name's is Jehovah Jireh which means provider. Our name is not nor is our employer named Jehovah Jireh.

The word *Trust* in Webster's means:

As a noun: Firm belief in the character, strength, or truth of someone or something. To be confident: Hope. Financial credit. (interesting!) A property interest held by one person or another for the benefit of another (bank etc). A combination of firms or corporations formed by a legal agreement and often held to reduce competition. Something held or managed by someone for the benefit of another. Responsibility for safety and well-being.

As a verb: To place confidence. DEPEND. To be confident. HOPE. To place in one's care of keeping. ENTRUST. To give financial credit to.

The definition of trust is imperative to grasp for our study on fear. You need to soak in the definition of trust. For if we are trusting in God for our well being, financial security, and if we have confidence and hope that God, Jehovah Jireh, is someone who is responsible for our safety and care then we have nothing to fear.

If we depend on God and if we believe that we are fully entrusted to God (meaning we believe we are His children and that He is fully capable of taking care of us) then we have nothing to fear. We can not and do not need to fear our circumstance or situation if we are children of God.

You say, "But you don't know what has happened to me?" That is true, I don't. I do know the God that I serve and I do know that He is able to free you from fear.

Fear is a feeling and it is also a spirit for the scriptures tell us that, "God has not given us a spirit of fear." That spirit of fear is from the adversary the devil and he is the one who uses fear to destroy our lives.

That is why David in the Psalms writes that although he may fear sometimes that He will trust in God. To combat fear and over come fear we must fully trust, (re-read your definition above) in God, Jehovah Jireh and not ourselves or our employer.

Memorize the definition of trust and know that beyond a shadow of a doubt that you can become fearless.

The Beginning of the Birth of the book

The time I will never forget:

To let go of fear you have to face the fear itself.

I met my dad for the first time in a prison cell in the fall of 2002. Meeting my dad in a prison was a challenging time and it took courage to face that fear.

That was the beginning of my voyage. Walking through prison doors and facing my dad at a prison cell changed my life forever. He sets the captives free. He sets all captives free-the ones behind the wall, (those in prison), and those outside the wall, (those in the world but who aren't really free.)

I had no clue where my dad was during my childhood and when I found out the truth-God took me on a voyage. The truth shall set you free and indeed it does.

The voyage that God has taken me on to be free from fear has taken many twists, turns, bumps, crashes and burns.

I have finally reached the destination. I call the destination: "The fearless fortress."

I have gone from fearful fallacy, (wrong thinking) and been led to the fearless One. God is a mighty fortress and a strong deliverer! He is our ultimate destination!

After meeting dad and going through some inner healing I thought I was free from all fear.

Yet fear crept in again in the Summer of 2008. I was a newlywed. Little did I know how the finances in the marriage would swallow me whole. The finances were bigger than I thought and fear began to consume me.

The devil knows our weakness. If we struggle with fear then he will do his best to attack us in our weakness. However praise God that God's strength is made perfect in weakness! God wants to use us in the very area we struggle the most! Praise the Lord.

It was hotter than blue blazes in North Carolina that Summer. It was also getting hot in our marriage!

I was out of work and my husband's business was not thriving. I had a restless night's sleep and when I woke I felt a demon of fear surrounding me. This feeling was different than anything I had ever experienced. I could not get out of my bed. It seemed fear had swallowed me alive. It was as though a demon was in the room and it was as big as a whale. That demon had swallowed me alive, so it seemed, just as Jonah had been swallowed alive by the whale.

When I began analyzing my thought process, I realized I was fearful of losing everything I owned. I call it, "fearful fallacy!"

Obviously I had gotten temporary insanity forgetting that God gives all we have to us and God can do what He wants! What we have is not really ours, yet, we all act like it is.

All we have been given is a gift from God and all we have is His for the scriptures are clear, "The earth is the Lord's and all that is in it."

We are living in a time where foreclosures seem unavoidable and many are filing bankruptcy. Many are afraid of losing it all. God encourages us to not be afraid.

To be afraid or not to be afraid, that is the question.

There is no condemnation in Christ. If you are afraid admit it. It's ok to admit our fear. Our God does not want us to be afraid and He desires us to be free from fear. It is hard to admit that first time that you are afraid. Once you do, healing begins.

Then, my worst and dreaded fear came true; my husband left me to sleep in another place for a few days. I had struggled with issues of abandonment prior to marriage and the enemy knew this and attacked our marriage.

It was then in the most fearful moments of my life this book came to life.

I began praying every single day before I got out of bed a small simple prayer, "Help Father, I am afraid." I didn't know how else to pray.

I had been a born again believer since I was a little girl. I knew how to pray bigger prayers than just help! Yet, I couldn't pray anything but *help!*

God the Father heard and helped.

I then began on a mission to search the scriptures to see what it said about fear. What I found is in this book.

Since my dad went to prison when I was a toddler, I did not have a father there to hold me in the middle of the night when I thought I had beasts under my bed. I did not have a dad there to tell me it would be ok when I was afraid.

To talk to God as a Father was something that I desperately needed. I also desperately needed Him to hear His little girl, although age 39, say, "Help Father, I'm Afraid." I needed my Father to hold me, wipe away my tears, and tell me it would be all right.

God gave me a love letter during this difficult time-a passage from every book of the bible, to help me with my fear. I have written that love letter to you, the one He gave to me. Then, I have taken each passage of scripture, from Genesis to Malachi the verses that God used to encourage me during my time of fear, and have broken them down into devotionals.

It is my prayer that this will help you to overcome your fear of losing it all, it is all His anyway and He gives, and He takes away. Blessed be the name of the Lord~

Prayer for you:
Lord Jesus Christ I come before you today and pray for every single person reading this book. I ask for you to give them peace where there is no peace. I ask Father that you would remove the heavy weight that is on their shoulders. I pray Lord that you would remove anything that hinders. Give them freedom from fear in their mind, will and emotions today. May they understand your will and purpose for their life and may all fear be gone from their life permanently in the name of Jesus Christ. Amen!

How to use this book

You can read a chapter a day for 39 days.

It is best however to do this book with a friend or bible study group. At the end of each chapter are questions and a personal quiet time challenge.

I would not suggest reading more than one chapter a day as you need to answer each question and take time out to do the quiet time.

It would be great if you had an accountability partner to help you during this study-someone you can trust and pray with.

If you choose to lead a "Help Lord, I'm Afraid" bible study group in your area please go through the study first before you lead a group. Help others in your group answer the questions honestly and do the quiet time.

Content

Day 1

Fear of the Future

Genesis 16: 7-9 The angel of the Lord found Hagar near a spring in the desert: it was the spring that is beside the road to Shur. And he said, "Hagar, servant of Sarai, where have you come from, and where are you going?" "I am running away from my mistress Sarai." She answered. Then the angel of the Lord told her, "Go back to your mistress and submit to her." The angel added, "I will so increase your descendants that they will be too numerous to count." (round one in the desert)

Genesis 16: 13 She gave this name to the Lord who spoke to her, "You are the God who sees me," for she said, "I have now seen the One who sees me."

Genesis 21:16-19 Then she went off and sat down nearby, about a bowshot away, for she thought, "I cannot watch the boy die." And as she sat there nearby, she began to sob. God heard the boy crying, and the angel of God called to Hagar from heaven and said to her, "What is the matter, Hagar? Do not be afraid; God has heard the boy crying as he lies there. Lift the boy up and take him by the hand, for I will make him into a great nation." Then God opened her eyes, and she saw a well of water. So she went and filled the skin with water and gave the boy a drink.

Round two in the desert, God *sees* you.

In the beginning of time in a land far away beside the road to Shur, a young teenage girl named Hagar was all alone in the dark desert of fear. She was in the darkest times of her life when she was in the desert, twice.

The story of Hagar is a timeless story of a woman filled with fear to a woman who becomes fearless.

Hagar was Abraham's maid-servant and Abraham's wife Sarai could not get pregnant. Sarai had waited ten years to get pregnant and decides to take matters into her own hands. She told her husband Abraham to sleep with her maid-servant so that perhaps she could have a family through her. Hagar became pregnant and began to despise Sarai. When Sarai began mistreating Hagar, she ran away to the desert fearful and pregnant.

Twice Hagar goes to the desert.

This is the first time she runs away into the desert. At this point she is pregnant. The second time she is sent away and her son Ishmael is with her.

The first time in Genesis 16 the angel of the Lord appears to Hagar and asks the young girl two very important questions.

"Hagar, where have you come from?" Sometimes we can't see the forest between the trees. It seems by the angels question that Hagar had not any thought about the place she had just left. Abraham was God's man. Abraham and God were tight. Abraham was the wealthiest man alive and he was the father of the faithful. Hagar had it made being in Abraham's house although she was being mistreated by another woman.

The second question is brilliant. I can only imagine and picture the angel clearing his throat and saying, "Excuse me, Hagar, have you given any thought to where you are going? You are young and pregnant. It's not safe for you to be out here in this dreadful vast desert. Do you have a plan where you will give birth to this child? Have you even thought about what will happen to you if you stay out here in this hot place?"

The young teenager yells, "I'm running away!"

Put your name in the blank. Picture yourself as Hagar. You have just run away from home and you are a young teen age girl all alone in the desert and you are pregnant. Picture yourself in that desert place. Maybe you are even there right now, not literally, but your soul feels like it is in a desert place and you do not know where you are going or where you have come from.

We've all been there. Some have run away from God. Some have run away from their troubles by drinking too much or doing drugs or getting into unhealthy relationships to numb their pain. Some have run away from home because they don't like their authority and ended up on the streets of Los Angeles alone and hungry and begin to do things that God had not planned for their life. Running away from our pain our hurt our troubles or our conflict never gets us to where God wants us.

The angel tells her to go back to Sarai, the very one who is mistreating her, and to submit to her authority. God has a plan and it is not Hagar's plan.

Many of us don't like to submit to our authority and we may have very good reasons. Until the last few months of my life I have struggled with submitting to authority.

When I was with Youth with a Mission God delivered me and healed me of past hurts from my authority. This issue was because my dad had been in prison my entire life and my mom worked three jobs and I rarely saw her. I struggled with respecting and obeying authority because my mom was not ever there, (physically because she had to work two and three jobs to put food on the table,) and dad was in prison. Not submitting to authority nor respecting authority has caused problems for me in jobs and in my marriage.

I don't think I am, "better than authority." My issue was that in my fearful fallacy I didn't really believe in my authority. I was afraid of abandonment and therefore many times I took matters into my own hands, much like Hagar. I ran and ran into the desert of fear. At times I ended up alone, abandoned, and afraid.

One of the reasons many of us don't submit to authority is because of a deep rooted issue of fear. It is a fear of losing control. If we have trusted God as our Savior, then He has full control of our life and we can trust in Him to do all things for our good, whether or not we like our authority or not. God is our authority if we are believers and He tells us to submit to our authority. If your authority is mistreating you, then submit to them as long as they don't ask you to sin. Allow God to work in your life and their life. Ask God what He wants you to learn during this difficult time. God is in the learning business and everything in our life happens for His purpose if we are called by God. God will work it out for good in His perfect timing.

Perhaps your authority in your past has hurt you physically or emotionally and you don't trust authority. Maybe your authority abused you as a child and you have deep wounds. Maybe you have been fired from many jobs and don't trust or respect authority of any kind.

Hagar did not want to submit to Sarai because she was being mistreated. However, this was God's plan for Hagar. God wanted Hagar to learn some things about her and about God. Once we learn to submit God's way, and pray for our authority, then God can get the glory and we can be free from fear of losing control of our life.

The angel of the Lord appears and minister's to Hagar during a fearful time. Hagar is pregnant and she has just run away without any thought to where she may be headed. She has no family near she has no one to comfort her and she has no money. An angel appears and tells her to go back and to submit to the very person that Hagar was running away from.

Why would God want Hagar to go back and submit to someone who was mis-treating her? God wanted Hagar to trust Him and God had a plan that would bring honor and glory to His name. God does things that are going to bring fame to His name and He is all about the Kingdom. For what we see on this earth is temporary and what lasts forever is what is unseen.

God saw Hagar fearful in the desert and I believe that desert represents her parched soul.

Hagar must have been afraid of being alone for the rest of her life. She was alone in her very own home for Abraham did not love her. Fear of loneliness plagued the young girl.

The desert she was in was not just a physical desert, but a spiritual desert. It has been said for believers that what happens in the natural also happens in the spiritual. The desert of fear in our soul is something many of us can understand. She needed someone to see past the obvious down deep into the parched desert places of her soul. She needed a Father to say to her, "I see you Hagar. Even though Abraham doesn't notice you, I notice you. My child, don't be afraid."

God the creator knew her inmost being intimately. The angels were sent to her by a loving heavenly Father who saw her soul crying out in the desert. The Lord knew she wanted to be noticed for who she really was, a woman who had longings and dreams in her heart.

In the middle of her pain and fear the angel of the Lord shows up to this young teenager and tells her to fear not. It was as though God Himself came down to earth and spoke to her. He penetrated Hagar's parched soul, with life.

Father God saw the pregnancy long before the fearful teenager saw God. The first time in the desert, while the girl was by a spring, the Lord approaches her.

God knew there was a son in her womb, long before he was even on the earth. (Jeremiah 29:11) God knew all about the teenager, where she was and His plan for her life.

The ancient of days calls out to us from the deep and into our soul even today. Just sit still and quiet long enough to hear God. You can hear Him deep down in the desert place of your soul. You can hear the quiet voice of God asking you, "Where have you come from? Where are you going?"

Maybe you don't know where you are going and maybe you don't know where you've come from. God wants you to ponder these two questions today. He longs for you to submit yourself to Him for He has a great plan for your life. If you don't have a plan for your life God is sending an angel to minister to you right now and the angel says to you, "Do you know where you are going?"

Just as God saw the young teen-ager in the desert both times God sees what has happened with the economy. He created each of us on the earth and He longs to fill our empty soul with life. God is not bound by the economy and if you are believer neither are you. God wants to impregnate you with a life giving dream! God wants you alive again! God wants that God-given dream to come to completion and He will provide.

The young maid-servant was running away from the life that God had laid out for her. Perhaps she was having an identity crisis. She could have secretly compared herself to her mistress. She had even fallen in love with Abraham and knew she couldn't have him. She needed to cry and let go of her pain. She needed someone to tell her to fear not.

Much like you and I would do Hagar ran away from her problems into the fearful hot desert. Picture the emptiness that she must have felt in her life living in that house with her mistress day after day being mistreated and longing for love. She wanted to get away from it all and there was no place to go where she could feel safe and warm. She started to run and once she did she could not stop running.

She must have ran and ran as far as she could with tears rolling down her face not being able to take it one more day in that tent. Suddenly, almost as dramatically as you might picture she falls down in the desert and begins to cry. Exhausted from her running she collapses in the dirt.

The bible tells us that we are all clay and made from the dust of the ground. Hagar collapses in the dirt and she must have felt like dirt herself.

When we are filled with fear we usually run to the very place that we think in our heart of hearts we really are. If we feel wretched we may run into a wretched relationship. If we feel like we are worth nothing we may drink or do drugs to numb our pain of feeling worthless. Hagar went to the lonely place of the desert and it was a picture of her heart and soul at that moment in time.

She had not gotten any loving attention from the man she loved. He did not have relations with her out of love, for his wife was the one who asked him to have relations with her. Nor had the young teenager gotten any positive attention from her mistress. Out in the desert it was as though she had finally been noticed by a loving man, who loved her for who she was, and where she was at emotionally and spiritually in her life. She was so exuberant about this, so she exclaims with delight, "You are the God who sees me!" "The God of the universe, the Creator, sees me out here in the middle of nowhere angry alone and bitter! God sees me and He even sent an angel to help me! God sees me. Finally, someone notices me!" "I am not invisible someone finally sees me for who I really am and loves me just the same."

The light finally came on and it was God's light shining down on Hagar.

The young girl goes back and submits to Sarai with confidence. God had seen her and she had exclaimed out loud in that desert that God the Almighty One had seen her! She also exclaims that she had seen God, the one true God, the loving God who noticed her. She had seen the truth, and the truth had set her free. She was free to obey God and go back and submit to her authority. She was filled with courage and power from the Holy Spirit.

This is what happened to Hagar in an instant with God in her life. She went from a fearful girl running away from home to a fearless, (free from fear and brave), young pregnant teenager and ready to submit to whatever Sarai tells her.

One fine day, a long time ago a young girl named Hagar, in a timeless moment of time found a loving God in the desert storm of her life. He met her right where she was, without judgment, without anger, and without shame.

A long time ago beside the road to Shur a young teenager named Hagar became free from fear. She put her trust in God. The one who took true notice of her, first!

She goes back to her home for a few years and is provided for and has all her needs met. She gives birth to a son, and Abraham does love his son as a father would love his son. It seems for a few years in time the young girl that was once afraid in the desert, has had a new found courage and strength that only a loving God could give her. She faces each day with strength from God and lives in the tent with her son Ishmael, and Abraham and Sarai.

It does not say that her life gets easier it only says that she went back and submitted to her mistress. Sarai was the authority over the maid-servant and God tells us all to submit to our authority. As challenging as this was, the young teenager did so fearlessly.

She could have dis-obeyed the angel of the Lord and kept on wandering around in the desert and given birth to Ishmael in the desert. Yet she goes back and submits and is provided for and gives birth to Ishmael in a place where his dad is.

Sarai becomes more jealous year after year and finally tells Abraham to send the young girl and little Ishmael on their way. It is clear that Sarai is the one that had the problem and not Hagar. Abraham does as his wife tells him and sends the young girl and Ishmael into the desert without a blueprint, without a road map, without a cell phone, without directions.

By the time the young teenager and her son wander to the desert place the young girl is so overcome with fear and grief she begins to sob. I am sure she had forgotten she had been here before for it had been several years since she had been in the desert.

She also forgot that a long time ago beside the road to Shur that she had given God a name and had exclaimed loudly,

"You are the God who sees me!"

She forgot for a brief moment in time that God had met with her personally and knew her name!

Have you trusted in God long ago for your financial security and well-being? Do you know beyond a shadow of a doubt that He has provided for you in ways that you have clearly seen in your past? However, you are now so overcome with fear of your financial situation that you have forgotten all that God has done for you? Have you seen God do healings in your life, but have forgotten that now? Have you seen God do marvelous things in your children's lives but are afraid that they won't make it in this tough economy? God is the same yesterday, today and forever!

It is time for you to remember what God has done for you and your family.

I imagine she did not want to be in that desert. For this time, Hagar wasn't running away! She was thrown out on the street! She was kicked out of her home because another woman was jealous of her. She had done all she was told to do, and yet Sarai got jealous and sent her away. She was minding her own business and living her life with a wealthy family, having all her needs met and now here she was in the desert and the water in the skin was gone.

It is not any wonder she was sobbing in the desert? She must have been sobbing those gut wrenching tears we all know about when we obey God and things don't turn out our own way.

She must have screamed in the middle of no where, "Why God why? I did what you told me to do, I submitted to her and she didn't like me anyway! That lady threw me out with a son all by myself!"

Hagar forgot the fine print and she forgot her God who sees her. The young girl also forgot that years before in the desert place that God had told her that she would have many descendants for she exclaims, "I can not watch the boy die here in this dreadful desert!"

She knew the fine print she had created the fine print herself but forgot it in her fear. Regardless of what God had promised her the first time around the desert she forgot what kind of relationship she had with God.

The second time around in the desert God sent another angel to minister to Hagar. The angel ministered to her right where she was sobbing by a well of water. Hagar had now given birth to God's dream, Ishmael, and she was sobbing those gutwrenching tears that all women know about after giving birth.

Her fear had now become magnified. Her fear was so magnified that all she could see was death. She no longer saw the God who she had once seen! The second time around after giving birth to a dream, Hagar was more afraid!

How many of you know that after giving birth to your dream that God has for you, you may experience fear and depression? How many times in our lives have we thought our children, ourselves, our dreams, our goals, or our plans would die even though God has promised them to us?

There poor single mom was in the middle of the desert with her son and her parched soul all over again. She had run out of water and she had run out of steam.

The bible tells us that the second time around God heard the *child's cry* and not Hagar's. God desires us to come to Him like a little child in faith believing that He is going to help us in the desert place of our soul.

After the angel ministers to the young teen-ager she wiped her away tears without tissues. Suddenly she notices a well of water in the desert and it was longing to give them drink! The bible says, *"After Hagar wipes her tears she sees the miracle, the well of water."* This makes me want to shout!

The well of water was there all along! The provision was there the whole entire time while she was sobbing her heart out.

That God that was hanging out with Hagar in the desert, the God who had already provided her provision, although she couldn't see it, is the same God that you and I have today. Our God doesn't change. He is the same! He has already provided for us, and we could be missing the well of water! If the water in the skin in your life is gone, stop crying now, and look up! He has your provision for you.

He saw her and all she had to do was stop sobbing, open her eyes and see the provision. In her fear and with her face down in her hands sobbing she did not notice God, but God noticed her.

Father God had already made a way for the mother and child when there seemed to be no way.

She had forgotten that she had named God, 'You are the God who sees!' God, the living water, was with Hagar, and her son, in the driest and most lonely place. He was providing for them exactly what they needed long before they even noticed. They needed water and that well was there the entire time.

When our soul is downcast we miss God. When we are consumed with fear and our problems we forget God and all that He has done for us in our past. When we are right in the middle of our newest dilemma we don't seem to remember that God is with us. What God has done for us in our past He can do more for us in our present and our future. God wanted Hagar to be consumed with Him, not her fear. The Father longs to be our all consuming fire and our Living Water. Your blessing could be right in front of you. Lift up your head and wipe away your tears with tissues and look ahead.

The creator sees your goals dreams and desires. God has created something magnificent for your life. God knows what is being birthed in your life, implanted in you. Go and seek Him and talk to Him about your life. Ask Him, "Where have I come from, and where am I going?"

If the desert of your soul is near death today know that God has living water for you. God wants you to birth something spectacular. Whatever the dream is that God has for you, His desire is that you carry it to completion.
If you don't know which way you are going or where you are headed, don't be afraid for God has a blueprint for your life and it comes with directions.

Look up and see God. God sees you. God has wells of water for you in the desert.

Questions:

1. Where have you come from?
2. Where are you going?
3. Are you pregnant with a dream?-If so, write the dream down
4. Have you forgotten what God has done for you in the past?
5. What has God promised you long ago that has not come to pass?
6. What could be the blessing in front of you?
7. What is your well of water in the desert?(your provision, that you just could not see before now?)
8. What in the past do you need to forget?
9. What do you need from God today?
10. If you could be anything, what would it be?
11. The fine print for Hagar's life was the promise God gave her. It was one verse, and one thing that God had said. Hagar forgot the fine print. What is the fine print of your life?
12. Do you think you will die before the promise in your life is fulfilled?
13. Do you feel alive?
14. How can you now, after studying about Hagar, change your thinking about God?
15. What negative thoughts and emotions do you need to let die?

Quiet Time:

Take some time to sit quiet in the desert of your soul, and listen to what God says to you. Ask Him to birth something miraculous in your life.

Day 2

Fear of Imprisonment of your own Fear

Exodus 23:30, "Little by little I will drive them out before you, until you have become fruitful enough to take possession of the land"

All I ever needed to know about fear I learned from a stark dreary Mongolian land and an emperor named Genghis Khan. What does Genghis Khan have to do with it? Bear with me and you will find out some things about Genghis Khan that you probably never knew.

It was the year 2,000. I left my ten year boyfriend, approximately 60 pairs of bright colorful shoes, my charming romantic apartment, and most of my belongings behind in boxes of packed up dreams.

The bitter, icy New Hampshire land that I had known for eight years was becoming a chilling memory. The cold New Hampshire winters had gotten to my soul. It was time to leave the Winter storm behind. I had become bitter in those winter years, not better. It was time to move forward towards God's purpose.

Little did I know that one year later I would be going to the Promised Land of Mongolia.

One year later, with a back pack, hiking boots and a bible in tow, I drove from Alabama to Texas to do some training with Youth with a Mission. I shared a small ranch home with 16 other people and one bathroom for three months. Then it was off to the stark, icy, cold bitter land of Mongolia.

The above scripture came alive for me during this time. Little did I know what that scripture would become my life verse.

The trip to Mongolia and studying about the life of Genghis Khan transformed my life.

I do not condone Genghis Khan's Buddhist religion. God does love and died for the Buddhist people. I am not an advocate of how Genghis Khan murdered people to get his point across.

A person, however, can learn about fear from the man Genghis Khan.

In the past there had been a void in my life. I did not know my real dad. My parents divorced when I was 8 months old and dad went to prison. I did not know exactly where my dad was until a few months before I went to Mongolia. We were reunited after I got back from Mongolia.

As a young girl growing up without a father I had no thoughts of a bright future. I did not have much direction for my life and felt locked up inside. I longed for a dad as most young girls do but I did not know what was needed most in my life. I was able to understand how an orphan without a dad might feel and what they might need. Children without a dad need to know a Father's love. It was because of my own childhood experiences, and the inner healing that Jesus died to give me, that I was able to be merciful to orphans in another country.

We landed in the middle of nowhere Mongolia with no vegetation as far as the eyes could see. It seemed we had landed on another planet.

We walked into get our one bag and there was virtually barrenness from the time we landed on the planet to the time we picked up our bag at the terminal to the rest of our time in that land.

There was nothing inside the airport. There was not a soda machine to get a drink, no restaurant in the airport to eat and no shops. We went to get our bag in the terminal, and we were completely mesmerized by the ambience.

We were led to a dark, dreary apartment building. Then we had to walk up about 100 stairs, to our Mongolian pent-house. There were no elevators in the Mongolian apartment, enormous building. We were filled with complete, utter shock. I had only been in Mongolia about four hours, and I was completely in shock by the lack that surrounded me.

We wanted a clean shower, a nice bed, and a good night sleep.

None of that happened. The apartment had roaches in it and the "bed" was as comfortable as a Mongolian bed could be. As I looked out the window of our apartment I felt a cloud of fear over that Mongolian land.

The next day we went to the Mongolian orphanage. The orphanage was something you would see in a Charles Dickens film. There were no Americanized windows in the orphanage and it was stale, dirty and lifeless.

Upon our entry the kids were eager and joyful to see us. When they each hugged us it seemed they never wanted to let us go.

During our time in Mongolia we also traveled to the mountains in Mongolia. We climbed and climbed and when I got to the top of the mountain I stood on top of the mountain, and breathed deeply and longingly and deeply looked over that Mongolian land. It seemed to represent the souls of the people of Mongolia. Stark, barren, empty, fearful, and gray was the Mongolian land. The Mongolian people were filled with emptiness, and a void that only a loving Father could fill. I could not help but cry out to the Lord, "I lift my eyes up unto the Mongolian mountains where does their help come from God? It has to come from you, and you alone."

God had really freed me from a cangue in my life, a Mongolian cangue of fear. It became my mission while I was in Mongolia to minister to others out of the same way that God had ministered to me in my life. I wanted to be used as a vessel to help others become free from their cangue of fear, and to this day this is still my mission.

Here I was a small town girl from the other side of the tracks in no where Alabama standing on a mountain in no where Mongolia. It was hard to fathom that now here I was, a long way from home, longing to somehow get the point across to the Mongolian people. I wanted to shout that God had a good plan for their life and that they did not need to fear!

The stark dreary Mongolian land is also a picture what many in America are going through. Many souls here in America right now are empty and barren and need the Lord to help set them free from a cangue of fear.

The people in Mongolia think that our lives are all like the life of movie stars. That is what they see and hear. As I got to know the Mongolian people I was able to share that my dad had gone to prison when I was a toddler and I had not met him. I shared that my mother worked three jobs to put food on the table and that life in America could also be hard. They shared with me about how hard life was in Mongolia. I realized that people all over the world are the same in their hearts. All people long for love and connection.

Just as the Mongolian people can not realize what we as Americans go through nor can we really realize or understand what it is the Mongolian people have to suffer. Only God is the One who can heal their land. We can not change what it is they struggle with we can only go in there and help as God would lead.

Daily we got to experience the Mongolian orphanage. As I ministered to the orphans at the orphanage God had me come to the strong conclusion that we are all orphans without a dad. The Mongolian souls needed a father. From America to Mongolia, the human soul cries out for a loving father.

The human soul is much like Hagar's was, "I just need someone, anyone, to notice me!"

A soul cries out from the deepest parts for peace and love from a father no matter where that soul is born. At certain times in our lives that love is precious when it is a pure love from our dad. If we do not receive that pure love from our earthly dad it can cause deep dark barrenness in our icy cold soul.

 Until we meet God face to face we may never know the real true pure love that can come from a loving Heavenly Father. Our earthly dads will let us down but God never will. Our earthly dads may to go prison or die or abandon us but God will never leave us nor will He forsake us.

Genghis Khan never knew his heavenly Father and lost his earthly one at the age of twelve.

The strongest Mongolian empire was founded by Genghis Khan in 1206. Genghis Khan was born in 1160, and he became emperor in 1206. He was 46 years old when he began to reign.

His life did not start out as a life filled with peace yet Genghis Khan had a strong desire to be a peacemaker. His goal to become a peacemaker began at the age of nine. With the terror and fear that he experienced as a young child his goal to want to be a peacemaker was vanquished by the enemy. The enemy comes to kill steal and destroy our lives from Mongolia to America. The devil is the destroyer of life and brings only death.

Jesus came to set us free from a cangue of fear and satan wants us to be bound up and locked in this cangue.

At 9 years old his parents had already decided who he would marry and he was delivered to her tribe, to live until he became the marital age-the ripe old age of 12. At that time, upon his return to his family, his dad was poisoned by his enemies, the Tatars. Upon returning home, he tried to claim his rightful position, as leader of the pack, but his dad's tribe refused to let him lead, because he was too young. Strange culture, at 12 he was old enough to marry, but not old enough to lead a tribe.

At 13 he was in a hunting accident with his half-brother, and that led to his half-brother's death. Now, that the tribe felt he was old enough, he assumed his rightful position as head of the household. He and his mother and brothers lived in poverty, living on wild fruit.

Young Genghis was captured and imprisoned in his teens and they put him in a cangue. A cangue is a large heavy flat board with a hole in the center big enough to hold a person's neck. They put the person in it and fasten it with locks around the neck and sometimes up further than the neck. The person is locked in this for days, sometimes months. Genghis Khan, a child, was locked in this. They did not feed him nor did they care for him. At times they would beat him and I won't go into the other details.

It has been said that a compassionate onlooker saw that young Genghis couldn't eat nor go to the bathroom and had other torture. The compassionate on-looker freed him!

I imagine young Genghis Khan locked up in this cangue crying out for his dad. He was just a little boy! He didn't ask for any of this. His dad had been killed by his enemies and these enemies are the ones who captured young Genghis. I imagine him crying out for his father to help him and crying out in the night that he missed his dad. As a young boy Genghis was not a murderer and he had no thought of killing people.

Yet the enemy came and destroyed this young boys' life. Fear destroyed Genghis Khan's life and the lives of hundreds of thousands other Mongolian people. This is the life that young Genghis had as a boy.

Do you feel as though you are in a cangue of fear? God is your compassionate on-looker and wants to free you.

This imprisonment and release is what led to Genghis Khan's ultimate goal to establish so-called 'peace' around its Mongolian borders. Young Genghis became fearful and began killing his dad's enemies to bring 'peace' to his territory.

It has been said that he began working hard and with a determination to bring, "peace." He ended up becoming a brutal murderer all because of fear and the enemy.

Genghis Khan grew the largest empire that Mongolia has ever had. The empire was based on fear. This is all just too sad. He could have been used as a man for the Kingdom of God only if someone had told him about Jesus Christ.

The enemy used fear to destroy a young child's life and that fear ruined Mongolia. It was fear that had destroyed the life of Genghis Khan and a nation.

Fear, if not dealt with in our lives, will eventually be used to not only hurt the lives of those around us and even people we may not even know.

Fear is a demon that needs to be destroyed out of each of our lives.

There is a strong sense of urgency that fear needs to be conquered in America. Fear is a powerful force of darkness and it needs to be conquered by the light and life of Jesus Christ. Jesus is more powerful than fear. You must recognize any part of fear that is in your life and allow Jesus to conquer it. Allow Him to lead you to Himself for He is fearless and He is a mighty fortress.

Light overcomes the darkness.

Genghis Khan thought he was establishing so called peace among the tribes that his dad loved and around the Mongolian borders. His twisted point of view was because of his abusive childhood and fear is what overcame young Genghis Khan. One can not excuse his behavior.

When you are in Mongolia there are statues and pictures of Genghis Khan. Yet the paintings are said to not be accurate. He is painted with dark hair and dark eyes yet in real life he had red hair and green eyes. It is said that Genghis died and some people had an image of darkness in their mind when they thought of Genghis. They took out the paint and paint brush and painted on the canvas what they saw in the man. They saw darkness and that is what they painted. They painted a canvas of fear when they painted him.

You are made in God's image and God has painted a picture of you. The picture painted of you is painted bright and you are on top of a mountain. There are flowers all around you on top of this mountain. The flowers are roses, lilies, and all your favorite flowers. The rainbow is above you and the glory of God fills the air. Smells of glorious flowers penetrate your soul in the painting and therefore your eyes are filled with joy from the One who is the joy-giver. You are looking up and God is looking down and He is singing. He is singing over you a song of delightful praise. It is the most glorious music you have ever heard. You are completely free in this painting-free from all fear. This is an accurate picture of how God sees you. God rejoices over you and loves you. You do not have to be locked up in your own fears any longer.

Despite his religious beliefs, Genghis Khan, one who had a rough up bringing, and one who had been imprisoned, with something locked around his neck for months, ended up as a child longing to establish so called peace. He had the largest empire the country has ever known. His empire was based on fear.

What led to Mongolia's downfall was fear and hate and a rapid conquering of other surrounding areas.

We can learn lessons from this Genghis Khan's life about fear. What made a young boy who wanted to have peace in his life become a murderer and kill his dad's enemies? Fear had consumed his life from the time he was a young boy and fear is what drove him to murder others until the time he died.

History tells us that when his successor came into power and acted hastily by conquering lands with speed that China wanted to go to war with Mongolia.

That war with China lasted 50 years and led to Mongolia's downfall.

God wants to remove our enemies and things that imprison us and He wants to do that little by little so that we can take possession of the land that He has for us. He wants us to bear fruit. We can not bear fruit, while we are bearing fear. We can not be in a hurry for the scriptures also tell us to be still and know that He is God.

Our country is living in a hurry and people get frustrated when they have to wait for anything. The hurry of life will cause us to miss what it is that God has for us. We all need to take time to slow down to see what it is that God has for us. We need to take our eyes off ourselves and our circumstances and ask God what

His purpose is for our life. We can only hear His voice when we are still.

Imagine if young Genghis had been a believer. He could have established a peaceful kingdom and helped to set others free from the grip of fear. Yet he ended up causing more fear because he became plagued by fear at a young age. Young Genghis was sick and had a disease called fear. Fear is a poisonous disease and if not dealt with in our lives it will destroy our lives.

As believers we have the One inside our heart who died for us to give us a life filled with peace and not fear.

If Genghis Khan had been a born again spirit filled believer he would have had eternal peace in his heart and would not have killed others to establish false peace around the borders. He could have been used as a man in God's army and been a powerful warrior for the Kingdom of God.

Satan comes to kill steal and destroy. God comes to bring life and it is His desire for us to be still, wait and be patient for what He has for us. He never wants us to take matters into our own hands because we are afraid. If we do this we are missing out on God's blessing and what He has for our lives.

Genghis Khan did not have an earthly dad from the time he was twelve years old. It seems that even today in Mongolia there are a lot of children without a dad and living in an orphanage. Mongolia needs to be delivered from a spirit of fear.

Until we come to meet God face to face we are all orphans. Until we meet God face to face our souls are stark and barren like the Mongolian desert.
Until we deal with our issue of fear we are a little child crying for our father, and locked up in a Mongolian cangue. After studying Genghis Khan and then going to the orphanage in Mongo-

lia I was determined to become a fearless woman, not a fearful woman.

It is my strong desire to empower others to live their lives as fearless women of God.
The children that I met in a Mongolian orphanage longed for love attention and time together. They had smiles on their faces as we painted their orphanage bright colors. I watched the transformation of the dreary orphanage to a life giving friendly orphanage. We all know in America what paint can do to transform a room. These children and adults had never seen such bright colorful paint in their lives.

I watched with delight how the children came and put their hands in paint. This bright red, orange, green and yellow paint was something they had never seen Their little Mongolian eyes filled with wide-eyed wonder, put their hands on the wall, and watched their little hand print become bright on that wall!

It was as though God was making a permanent mark on that wall at the orphanage. The writing on the wall from God to those children was, "I will never leave you nor will I forsake you. I have a bright future for you if you just put your trust in me and not fear."

To this day, the children's bright colored hand prints remain an image in my mind. Yet, in reality, those hand prints are permanent, on the wall, at the orphanage of Mongolia. Those children's handprints and lives are permanently in God's heart and mind. He longs to bring them peace!

Once we come and meet Jesus face to face He has us. Our lives are His and our little hands can grab His hand and He can lead us to where He wants us to go. He has a colorful, wide-eyed wonder life for all of us who are His. The dreariness, and the dark, dreary, stark land that people have today in America, and round the world, is because of an enemy, and his name is satan. God is the life giver and the devil brings death.

Since our soul lasts forever then it makes perfect sense that God hears the cries from our soul. From Hagar in the desert to a Mongolian desert, to an American culture struggling in the economy, God hears our cries.

It seemed those little Mongolian children had a faith that we adults don't grasp. They did not seem afraid although there was starvation, and lack of clean water at that orphanage. They had no toys to play with, no toilet paper in the bathroom, and no TV to watch.

They had no ice cream to eat, no snack for snack time, and not many choices for food.

Yet, they were focused on the cheery, not the dreary. For a time-less moment in time, these little ones were playing with paint. They had forgotten all their worries, and were extremely joyful! Oh, the wonder of it all, in a Mongolian orphanage.

It seemed those children were thankful for bright colored paint, and us being there, more than being consumed with their fear. They were caught up in the delightful moment of bright joy. All fear was gone for those days in the Mongolian orphanage for those children.

There was another day where we had a basin, and soap to clean the children. After we cleaned the children, we wanted to paint their fingernails. The little boys even wanted nail polish on their hands. There were also adult Mongolian ladies who had never seen bright nail polish, and were just like us in America, waiting in line to get their nails done. Yet it was at an orphanage and not a spa.

There are no beauty salons in Mongolia where the ladies can get a manicure. The little boys of that orphanage did not know any better so we did put nail polish on their tiny finger nails and they were filled with joy.

God was with me in a Mongolian Orphanage, and God was longing for those Mongolian children to have love, peace and joy in their life. God was the painter of that orphanage. God was the one who brought the paint. God was the one who longed to free them from their own personal cangue in Mongolia.

Those Mongolian children are now eight years older. Some have been released and others are still in that orphanage. Yet, I know, beyond a shadow of a doubt, that they have not forgotten the bright colors, and the bright day, eight years ago, when men and women from America came and showed them God's joy.

God wants to be your loving Father. It is His desire to release you from your orphanage and cangue of fear. He longs for you to have joy and be free from your fears!

He holds the key to free you from your fears.

Have you heard that fear is false evidence appearing real?
Genghis Khan may have been the strongest, most powerful emperor that Mongolia has ever known and sadly it was twisted by an enemy-the evil one.

Jesus Christ is the Almighty Emperor. He wants to live in you and in me and conquer all fear in our lives and around our borders!

God the almighty Emperor wants us to have a fruit filled life of peace. The loving and perfect Almighty Emperor who died on the cross over 2,000 years ago to give us peace wants to conquer fear in your life.

He wants to establish peace in your heart and around your borders.

He does not want you in the desert of Mongolia wandering around in a dark, stark, dreary land. He does not want us locked up to our necks in a cangue of fear. He wants to have us conquer all fear so that we can be fearless men and fearless women of the Almighty Emperor. He then wants to use us to bring peace to a fearful world out there.

He desires to drive out things in your heart and life that do not belong there so that you can become fruitful enough to take possession of the land!

The fruit of the spirit is love, joy, peace, patience, kindness, goodness, gentleness, faithfulness, and self-control. He longs to remove hate so that you can have love. He longs to remove sadness so that you can have joy. He longs to remove impatience so that you can have patience. He longs to remove the bad and ugly out of your life so that you can have goodness. He longs to remove the people that are mean to you and longs to remove the mean ness out of your life so that you can have kindness in your heart. He longs to remove the stony harshness cold and bitter parts of your soul so that you will be a gentle person. He longs to remove dis-order, unfaithfulness out of your life so that you can be faithful not only to Him but to yourself, your finances, your life, your job, and all that He has given to you. He longs to remove your out of control life and self so that you can have more self-control in your life.

With God, the almighty Emperor living inside us, we can become people set free from fear and establish peace in our soul and around our borders.

We need to give our heaviness to Jesus so that He can bear our burden of fear so that we can bear fruit. We need to become peace-makers and not be fear-mongers.
God has more for you than you know. Little by little He is driving things out of your life that do not need to be there so you can become fruitful enough to take possession of all He has for you.

If Genghis Khan, without God in his life, can establish what he thinks is peace and have the greatest empire that Mongolia has ever known then how much more can the Almighty Emperor Jesus Christ do in the lives of the children in the Mongolian Orphanage and your life and mine?

Peace is the fruitful land that God wants you to possess. He is your compassionate on-looker today. He desires to release you from your cangue of fear.

All we have to do is cry out, "Help Father, I'm afraid." The Almighty Emperor will hear, answer and conquer. He will answer lovingly, purely, and righteously.

All I ever learned about peace, I learned from the almighty Emperor Father Jesus.

Questions:

1. What is your biggest fear?
2. Are you bearing fruit?
3. What does fruit look like to you?
4. How is your soul?
5. What land do you desire to possess?
6. What is your big, hairy dream?
7. Do you have idols in your life?
8. What idols do you need to get rid of?
9. Are you in a Mongolian wasteland?
10. Are you locked up in a cangue?
11. How can you become permanently delivered from fear?
12. If you were a fruit, what would you be?
13. What is your focus?
14. What do you see in your life?
15. What consumes your soul (mind will emotions?)
16. What is false in your life that appears real to you?
17. What do you believe about God?
18. What needs to be driven out of your life?

19. What can you learn from Genghis Khan?

Quiet Time:
 Talk to the Lord, and tell Him how you feel. If you feel you are locked up in a cangue, tell him. Ask Him to be the one who is compassionate enough to release you.

Day 3

Fear of the Beasts

Leviticus 3: 6: I will grant peace in the land, and you will lie down and no one will make you afraid. I will remove savage beasts from the land, and the sword will not pass through your country.

It was the same dream. I had been running in place for so long and it was dark all around me. No one could hear me when I screamed. Someone was chasing me and I did not know who it was. Whatever it was that was chasing me was invisible. Suddenly I woke up. It had been a nightmare.

I had that recurring nightmare for many years until the day that I met my dad in a prison cell in the fall of 2002.

God your Father wants to grant you peace and meet you face to face. You don't have to work hard to get this peace. It is a gift from your heavenly Father to you.

When God spoke this to the Israelites in Leviticus their land was in the desert and they had already been in that desert for many years. God under the new covenant dwells in your heart and He desires the land of your heart to experience peaceful waterfalls daily.

At night when you lie down it is not His will for you to have nightmares. If you are having nightmares about losing it all say a simple prayer, "Help Lord, I'm afraid." He will answer that prayer and give you peace. There are no savage beasts under your bed. The savage beasts have been removed by your Father.

Remember, a long time ago, when you called to Him in the night and He was there. He is always there for you.

When you meet your Father face to face all fear is gone vanquished and removed.

A grant is a gift freely given to you. In today's society we can apply for many different grants. People do research for the grant they want and fill out a large amount of paperwork, and, if approved, they get the grant. Show me the money is what people are crying out from their heart when filling out this pile of paperwork.

This grant of peace from God is a free gift and there is no paperwork involved. My friend, you are already approved! You just have to be open and receive the grant in your heart. "Show me the peace," is what we as believers can say to God when we are afraid and want a grant!

<u>The word grant in the Hebrew language means:</u>
To give, used with great latitude of application, add, apply, appoint, ascribe, assign, avenge, be healed, bestow, bring forth, hither, cast deliver, direct, distribute, do, doubtless, without fail, fasten, frame, get, give forth, have indeed, give, leave, lend, let out, lift up, make, occupy, offer, ordain, pay, perform, place, pour, print, put forth, recompense, render, requite, restore, send out, set forth, shoot forth, sing, submit, suffer, surely, take, thrust, trade, turn, utter, weep, willingly, withdraw, would to God, yield

God wants to give you a great latitude of peace. God has done the paperwork for you. He desires to appoint, assign, and bestow peace all over you. He wants to deliver peace to you, as someone delivers a Federal Express package to your door. He wants to lift you up with peace, to restore you unto peace, and for you to yield to peace. He longs for you to bathe in a pool of peace and has it in His heart to pour out a waterfall, an endless supply, of peace all over you.

The word beasts in the Hebrew language has different meanings in the book of Leviticus means: *Behemah: A dumb beast, a large quadruped animal, or cattle.*

It is God's desire for anything or anyone that is coming after you to be destroyed. God desires the many problems that you have that are making you afraid to be conquered. If you feel threatened today by a beastly enemy don't fear. God is on your side and is the One to avenge you.

Don't let the beasts of your life control your destiny. You choose to fear or not to fear. Fear is not something that just comes upon you one day while you are minding your own business. Fear is a result of wrong thinking mindsets, and negative emotions in our life. Fear is not something abstract it is something concrete. Do not let fear happen to you. Allow God in your life so you and God can happen to fear and conquer it. To fear, or not to fear, that is the question.

Don't let the invisible enemy of fear chase you in the dark and make you fearful!

The dumb beasts that you have had in your life, whether that is dumb mistakes or dumb decisions or dumb deals, can not make you afraid or control you any longer.

Get rid of the condemnation of the so called dumb mistakes and dumb wheals and deals you have made in your life. Do not let them ruin you or make you afraid. Embrace the new life that God has for you and this new life is a life filled with an abundance of peace.

If those strong, type a personalities have tried to control you (and I am a mix of type a and type b) and you have allowed them to control you, let it go! They can not control you any longer. Submit all of your pain to the Lord and allow Him to free you from controlling personalities. Ask Him to allow you the freedom to be at peace with all people and to allow Him to have charge over your decisions. Those strong personalities can not try to control your life any longer for the God of peace longs to have a relationship with you where He helps you make your decisions in peace. You do not have to worry about what others think. You can listen to their advice but you don't have to do what they say, and you don't have to tolerate manipulation. You only have to do what God says to you.

If you are having a struggle controlling your appetite, for one of the meaning of the word beasts is appetite, ask God to help you for He does not want food controlling your life. He wants that savage beast of over eating to go away permanently so that you can replace that over eating with His peaceful food and that is His word of life.

Maybe all of this is new to you, that having peace in your life is a choice and that God wants to literally grant it to you freely without charge.

Corrie ten Boom's life story, <u>The Hiding Place</u> is a must read.
Corrie was a lady that was captured by the Nazis and put in the concentration camp. Her entire family was captured because they had hid some of the Jews.

Corrie's sister was in the concentration camp also, and she complained about the fleas. Corrie had said to her younger sister, "Thank God for the fleas. Give thanks to God in all things."

In the end, after the war was over and Corrie was traveling the world preaching the gospel, she ran into one of the guards that had tortured her sister in the concentration camp. Corrie asked him why the guards never came down to their cell and his answer was 'because of the fleas.'

Many years prior to this her sister could not give thanks for the fleas. Corrie had a bible in her cell and they were able to read it and talk about the things of God. It was because of the fleas they were able to do this. No one but God knew this at that time.

How can Corrie be peaceful about the fleas and her sister be annoyed by them? It is called choice. How can one person be in the same situation and have a completely different outlook, attitude, and response during trying times?

God granted peace to Corrie in that concentration camp. Corrie received the grant of peace. She opened the goods and the peace reigned in her heart. That grant of peace was available to Corrie's sister also, but Corrie's sister didn't open the goods. She chose to focus on the fleas. Corrie, the one who had been granted peace is the one who survived the camp and her sister died.

If fear is the savage beast in your life that consumes you today, then realize that it is also spilling out onto your family, friends and those around you. Fear comes out of you in your attitudes, decisions and actions. Fear can eat you up inside and it is poisonous.

Fear is a savage beast that can consume, kill and destroy, and fear is what needs to be destroyed in all our lives.

Think about the fact that fear comes from our thoughts. Faith also comes from our thoughts. Would you rather have fear or faith? Would you rather have fear or peace?
If you lose your job you can be afraid that you won't get another one, or you can have the faith that you will have one because God is your provider. You have the ability to choose fear or faith.

Help Father, I'm afraid is a simple prayer you can pray and God will grant you peace in your land and remove all the savage beasts that are under your bed.

Questions:

1. Have you ever considered that fear affects not only you, but those around you?
2. What are the fleas in your life that you can not be thankful for?
3. What are you hiding from?
4. What is a grant of peace worth to you?
5. What has been granted to you?
6. What have you granted yourself?
7. Do you 'feel worthy'?
8. How does God see you?
9. How do you see yourself?
10. What are the savage beasts under your bed that plague you?
11. Do you have peace?
12. Do you want peace?
13. What does peace look like to you?
14. What is your definition of peace?
15. What was your childhood like?
16. Can you forget about your childhood?
17. How can you conquer the savage beasts under your bed?
18. Who is the big savage beast that you may fear?
19. How can you begin to create peace in your life?

Quiet Time:

Talk to God about peace. Share with Him pains from childhood. Ask Him to give you permanent peace that can only come from Him. Ask Him to show you the truth about yourself. Ask Him to help you to be thankful for the fleas of this life!

Day 4

Fear of Missing God's Grace

Numbers 6:24-26 The Lord bless you and keep you, the Lord make his face shine upon you, and be gracious to you, the Lord turn his face toward you and give you peace.

Peace and grace are in the Father's face. Show me the grace.

Whenever I visit my dad at the prison cell in Georgia he is delighted and peaceful to see me. We talk hug, visit, cry, and we have peace. There is peace of a Father's love towards his child that is evident every visit to that prison. There is never a worry in my dad's face when his daughter comes.

There is never a worry in my face. If my dad could do anything in the world for me he would. He would give me a million dollars if he had it.
This is from a man inside a prison.

My dad and I sit face to face in the lobby with a small table between us and when I look at my dad's face, I see my reflection. I am the splitting image of my father.

The peace that we have now is something that I did not have as a child from my dad. I did not know him as a little girl so I could not even fathom that meeting him would bring me peace. Yet in God's will and divine plan He had me meet my dad face to face and my dad has been peaceful ever since that meeting.

One day, I went to the prison and after checking in there was a man that approached me inside the prison and said, "You must be Mike's daughter, you look just like him. I just wanted to let you know that since he has met you he has slept better than he has in years."

My dad finally had peace of mind after meeting his daughter. Now that peace and grace was extended and given to me every time we visited. He never asks about my past, my sins or my mistakes. He just longs to sit with me and listen to whatever it is I have to say. He talks and shares with me many details of his life in prison. Conversations are filled with grace and peace because forgiveness has happened between the two of us. There is not any condemnation from either of us in our conversations and the conversations are always positive up beat and filled with love. If a man in prison knows how to extend grace and peace to his daughter how much more does the Heavenly Father wants to give that to you.

The only thing my dad does lecture me on is that if I do not answer his letters in a timely manner. When I visit him he will say, 'Now honey I know you're busy but please keep writing me, I love reading your letters.' He wants communication and connection with me. God wants the same from you.

This relationship that I have with dad is not something either one of us deserve. Dad committed a crime and I had anger and un-forgiveness for years towards this man I did not know. Grace means unmerited favor which is something given to us that we don't deserve. You don't have to earn grace nor do you have to earn peace with God. God has paid it all when He sent His son Jesus to die on the cross for our sins and the only thing you must do is believe the Son.

The way to get to the Father is through the Son.

The same way it is with an earthly dad. The way to get to my dad's heart is through me.

Your Heavenly Father's face is towards you, not behind you or away from you. He is face to face with you and His face is a loving face of peace and grace every time He looks at you.

Long before my dad and I met at that prison cell he had been praying for me for many years and I did not know it until I met him face to face. Your Father, God is looking toward you and is sending you this message of grace and peace. He has been thinking of you and missing you all these years if you have not opened up your heart to Him. He misses you also if you have not been in touch for a while.

People can tell a lot from your countenance. It has been proven that body language communicates more than our words. Your countenance speaks volumes to others. Your countenance is a direct reflection of what is deep inside you. If you know God intimately then your countenance can become that of the Father's face. You can continuously offer others grace and peace daily when you experience true peace and grace from the Father. Your relationships with family, co-workers and customers can be filled with peace and grace.

Imagine having peaceful and grace giving days every day of your life, even on Monday. If you desire to give a gift to someone today, then grace is something many would love to receive. Giving grace to someone is challenging at first because that is something they may not deserve. The next time you are in a fight with your spouse, or having a conflict at work, try praying for that person regularly. Smile at them when you don't feel like it. Take simple steps in your life to begin to experience giving away peace and grace. The more you pray for grace and peace in your life from God the more you can give that away to others.

It has been said if you want love then give it away and the same is true with grace and peace. Prayer is the key to open your heart so that you can receive grace and peace from God. You must ask Him daily for this even when you think you don't deserve it.

If you are afraid today your face may not look peaceful. Your face may look sad, bewildered, and confused. You could be frowning or crying all the time. You could have red eyes because of the tears. Your face may have even aged because of your sobbing.

If God is your Father, you are His child and you are made in His image. When you look in your mirror, crying, then dry your eyes, and freshen up your face. Look at the beautiful reflection in the mirror of the Father's face in your eyes. His face is a peaceful face. He has a face of calm.

He looks at you this way and wants that peace all over your face. He wants you to shine in this world and spread that peace to others. You are His child and you are the splitting image of your Father. May God, the grace giver, give you grace.

God wants grace in your face.

Do not be afraid. May the Lord bless you, keep you, and make His face shine upon you and give you peace.

Questions:

1. What is God speaking to you right now?
2. How can you have a moment by moment awareness of your Father God?
3. Did you know that you are the splitting image of your Father God?
4. How can knowing this change your perspective, daily?
5. How can you begin to look more and more like your Father God?
6. Do you need to wash your face, and clean up a bit?
7. What needs to be freshened up in your life?
8. Do you consider God's face towards you?
9. What was your earthly father like?
10. Do you need some healing in the area of you and your earthly Father?
11. Are you a shining star right now?
12. Do you want to become a shining star for God?
13. What action can you begin to take that will begin to make you a superstar for God?
14. Are you dazed and confused?
15. How can you get rid of all confusion?
16. What does your face look like on a regular basis? If you don't know, ask your closest friend
17. How do you want your face to look, always?
18. How can you make a conscious effort to have your face looking great every day?
19. How is your countenance?
20. How can you create a better countenance for yourself?

Quiet Time:

Talk to God about your countenance. Share with Him that you long for His grace in your face. Tell Him you want to be a beautiful reflection of His glory. Ask Him for forgiveness for all the times in your life when your countenance towards others was not the way He would have it to be.

Day 5

Fear of Getting No-Where

Deuteronomy 1:31 and in the desert, there you saw how the Lord your God carried you, as a father carries his son, all the way you went until you reached this place."

A re you pulling your own little red wagon?
I wonder whose brilliant mind came up with that expression.
If you try to pull your own little red wagon, it won't get you too far. Picture yourself sitting in a little red wagon and taking the handle and trying to make it go. How challenging is that? Does the wagon move? Does the wagon go very far? Do you go very far? We all need to be delivered from the person that told us, "Pull your own little red wagon." We need our inside soul to be set free from trying to do it all on our own. We need that image out of our mind.

We can not do anything without Jesus. We can not even breathe without Him. We can not pull our own little red wagon.

The Israelites were a people group that had been slaves for 400 years, and then God delivered them, by sending them a deliverer named Moses. Then, it took the Israelites 40 years to make an eleven day trip from where they had been in a slave camp, to the promised, fruit bearing land God had promised.

God wants to pull your little red wagon. God wants to carry you.

Many years ago, I watched a DVD inspired by a man who has a paraplegic son. His son had always wanted to be in a triathlon, the Iron Man. So the father and his son, trained. The Father takes his son on the bike, swim and run. While they are swimming, the son is in a boat in the ocean, while the dad is pulling him. While they are running, the dad carries him. While they are on the bike, the dad pedals, while the son sits on the back of the bike and enjoys the scenery.

The dad carries his son, while running, across the finish line. The crowd cheers, and weeps.

The song playing during this video is called My Redeemer Lives.

We all want a championship life. We can all be champions as believers. Do you think for one minute during the Iron Man that the son had any doubt they would finish the race, and get to the finish line? Through the video you see a sparkle in the son's eye. You see the son smile and you see the determination as the father carries and pulls his son.

God, your Redeemer Lives. He is carrying you to places you can not see. He is pulling you through life's journey. God is pedaling you up through the mountains and sometimes down into the Valleys of life. He wants you to enjoy the view and trust in Him to get you to the finish line. He is in business to take you home.

He is taking you through this life to your finish line, to your destiny. He desires to make your dreams come true and provide what you need to have them. It pleased this father to carry his son to the finish line. It pleases the Heavenly Father to carry you.

If you trust Him with a surrendered heart, mind, and soul, then you will not fear. Trying to pull your own little red wagon through your life is exhausting, and lonely.

You may not be able to see in front of you, nor can you see where God is taking you. Relax, enjoy the journey and the scenery. He is taking you places where you have never gone before and He is pulling you, cycling you, and carrying you across the finish line, with determination and love in His eyes.

He just wants you to sit back and enjoy the ride.

If you feel handicapped today, and we all are in many ways, trust your Father. Let Him carry you. Surrender your plans, your agendas, and your life. He will take you on a mesmerizing journey. Be like that son on the back of the bike during the Iron Man, looking at the beautiful mountains pass him by, as he rides on the back of the bike with his dad with a sparkle in his eye.

God wants to pull you in the boat in the ocean, and take you on a deep swim. He wants you to ride the waves of your life with him. He doesn't want you to struggle anymore, trying to do it all on your own, pulling yourself.

He wants you to complete the Iron Man of life while He carries you. He wants you to go through life with a sparkle in your eye!

You do not have to pull your own little red wagon anymore.

Questions:

1. Who carries you?
2. Are you carrying a heavy burden on your back?
3. Are you carrying yourself?
4. What is pulling you to and fro in your life?
5. Are you sitting back, enjoying the scenery?
6. What scenery would you like to look at, always?
7. What do you want to complete in your life?
8. Where do you want to end up in your life?
9. How do you plan to get there?
10. Are you pulling your own little red wagon?
11. How can God start to pull your little red wagon for you?
12. How far do you want to travel in your life?
13. How far do you think you can go?
14. Do you 'feel handicapped' today?
15. Do you think you can complete what you have started?
16. How can you finish the race before you?
17. What would your dream race be, and where would it be?
18. If you could accomplish anything in your life time, what would it be?
19. If you could ask Father God for one thing, one wish, one dream, what would it be?
20. What have you always wanted to do?

Quiet time:

Ask God to help you to finish what you have started that He has asked of you. Ask Him to carry you through to the finish line. Share with Him your dream scenery and tell Him that this is what you long for your soul to look like. Tell Him that you are tired of pulling your own little red wagon and you need Him to pull it for you.
If you feel, 'handicapped' ask God to use your handicaps for His glory and purpose.

Day 6

Fear of being Alone

Joshua 1:9 "Have I not commanded you be strong and courageous. Do not be terrified; do not be discouraged, for the Lord your God will be with you where ever you go."

God wants to be your commanding officer. God tells Joshua three times to be strong and courageous. I have heard pastors preach that when God is trying to get your attention, He repeats Himself.

Moses, the Israelites leader had died, and it was time for them to cross the Jordan and enter the Promised Land. God was raising up a new leader, Joshua. It is interesting that the Lord would tell Joshua to not be terrified. Not just scared or a little shaky or a little frightened, but terrified. Joshua's childhood playground had been a slave camp and then his teenage days were spent hunting in a desert. He had now entered into the Promised land that God had promised the Israelites and was about to conquer Jericho.

Joshua had witnessed all the miracles that God performed for the Israelites in the wilderness. He had seen Moses lead who had been the wisest leader the Israelites had ever known. He knew the power of God out of a burning bush. For God had appeared to Moses in a burning bush in the wilderness. He knew of God's glory, he had witnessed God's glory. He witnessed water coming out of a rock, and the Red Sea parting so millions of people could cross on dry ground.

Joshua knew the power of Almighty God.

Yet, He was still terrified.

God used the word, commanded. God commanded Joshua to be strong and courageous. Command is a strong word, so is terrified.

God commanded his son, Joshua, to not be terrified. It was not just a suggestion, it was a command. It was a duty for Joshua to not be terrified. It was as though a commander in the officer of the Army had said, "Joshua, don't be terrified." God consoles Joshua at the end by saying, "I will be with you wherever you go."

From a command to a consolation is how God dealt with His terrifying child.

In studying the word commander, there are many interesting facts.

I don't know if you have heard of the ICS, Incident Command System. This Incident Command System was founded in the 1970's after fires in California consumed hundreds of people and they all died. Several people got together and formed this group. This group has many different functions. Part of the group's agenda is to meet complex needs of people in an area when there are dangerous situations.

God wants to be our ICS, and meet all of our complex needs especially when we are in a dangerous situation. That dangerous situation could be anything that killing us financially, spiritually or otherwise. The dangerous situation could also be anything that is taking God's place in our life. It could be a false idol in our life, or looking for love in all the wrong places. God says, "Danger, Danger, your commanding officer is here, and I command you to be strong and courageous, I am with you. I am here to rescue you from danger. You will not die in this fire!"

If you are in the fire today then praise God because your commanding officer is with you now. He is going to rescue you from the most dangerous of situations and the fire will not choke you to death. Your financial fire is nothing to God who has all power to deliver you from the fire. Your fiery relationship is not what God wants for your life and God says, "danger, danger get out while you still can." Or, God could be saying, "Danger, danger I want you to notice me and praise me during this difficult fiery situation. I want to re-fine you in the refiner's fire so that you become pure gold." For you to be re-fined as pure gold in this fiery situation you must focus on me and praise me during these trying times.

You have probably heard how gold becomes pure is through the fire. If you desire to be of pure gold then you are going to have to go through the fire. Allow the commanding officer of your life to remove all impurities from your life and consume you so that you become as pure gold.

I have seen God do many miracles in my own life. I have seen Him provide for me while I was raising funds for the mission field. I had seen my mother work 3 jobs to put food on the table, while we got no child support from dad because he was in prison. Yet, God provided. He provided food every day of my life when I was a child, and He provided funds for me to get to Mongolia, India, and many other places around the world. God never fails and He continues to provide for me as a loving Father does for His child. I have been laid off and let go from many jobs in my life and watched God take care of my every need. We may not know how God will provide, nor do we know the future, but God the Father is already in your future. God knows how He is going to take care of your needs.

I have also seen Him remove relationships that were not good for me and at the time it was heart wrenching to watch that relationship die. I have had loved ones in my life pass away. I have lost friends through the years and I have made bad choices in my past. God has used each and every situation in my life to re-fine me in the fire. The commanding officer of my life has done what is good for His daughter because He loves me. At the time I may not have seen what He was doing, but now I see clearly all that He has done in my life. As we look back over our lives we can see God's hand in it and that can encourage us to move forward without fear!

God has a standard of living for His children. God's standard is for us to be strong and courageous. It is our duty to our God, our country and our fellow man.
Imagine if we had a world filled with bravery. What a wonderful life it would be on this earth living around brave men and women.

The Muslim faith even has a title for people in a high position. That title is, "Commander of the faithful."

The Sovereign Military Order of Malta is a chivalric order. This order was founded in the year 1080 in Jerusalem. It is a Christian order where Christians were to help pilgrims that were sick and poor on their pilgrimage to the Holy Land. There is a title in this order called Military Knight Commander. This position is about the highest position you can go. Back in the day, this Knight sat on a beautiful, gold, throne. You can see pictures of this in the online encyclopedia.

God is your commanding Military Knight and He says to you today, "Be strong and courageous."

The world needs one less fearful, terrified person. Let that person be you.

If you are God's child, you have someone higher and stronger than the Military Knight Commander living inside you. He longs to help you in your pilgrimage.

God is with you. Be strong and courageous wherever you go. It takes courage to face each day when you are facing many trials. It also takes courage to rise above the painful situation you may be facing. You will not fail, you will prevail. You are not alone, Almighty God is with you. He is more powerful and able to deliver you than anyone on this planet.

You will prevail in this pilgrimage because God is your Commanding officer.

Questions

1. Who is your commanding officer?
2. If the commanding officer in your life is you what do you tell yourself?
3. If the commanding officer in your life is your boss, what do you hear from the constantly?
4. If the commanding officer in your life is your spouse, what do they tell you to do?
5. If the commanding officer in your life is your parent, how do they talk to you?
6. Who consoles you?
7. Do you feel consoled in your terror?
8. Are you terrified of something today?
9. Do you want to be the one less fearful person in the world?
10. Have you ever thought of God as a commanding officer?
11. Have you ever thought that you are in God's army?
12. How can you be a better soldier for God?
13. How does your environment affect you?
14. How can you create a better environment for yourself?
15. How can you become courageous?
16. How can you begin today to gain strength from God daily in your life?
17. What do you need from God right now?
18. What command do you need from God that will change your life?

Quiet Time:

Talk to God and ask Him to be your commanding officer. Share with Him your greatest needs. Ask Him to help you be courageous.

Write out a commandment from God to yourself.

Day 7

Fear of Oppression

Judges 3:9-11 But when they cried out to the Lord, he raised up for them a deliverer, Othniel son of Kenaz, Caleb's younger brother, who saved them. The Spirit of the Lord came upon him, so that he became Israel's judge and went to war. The Lord gave Cushan-Rishathaim king of Aram into the hands of Othniel, who overpowered him. So the land had peace for forty years, until Othniel son of Kenaz died.

A long time ago in the land of Egypt a man named Caleb was born in a slave camp. He, along with millions of other Israelites were slaves and mis-treated by harsh task-masters.

One day a man named Moses became their deliverer and delivered them from the slave camp and left the slave camp with the hopes of a better life. They wandered in the wilderness for forty long years and many of them died. Caleb's younger brother Othniel was born in the wilderness. He was a man who deeply loved God, despite his up-bringing, surroundings or circumstances. Neither of them complained about eating manna every single day, as the other Israelites did.

Caleb had been highly favored of the Lord and his younger brother had been with Caleb through the many years in the wilderness watching God perform many miracles. They both grew into strong men who ended up conquering lands and many territories with their friend Joshua. They both were from a line of men who had learned to conquer lands and survive the wilderness. These men were hunters and had plenty of survival skills.

Not much is mentioned about Othniel in the scriptures, yet Othniel was a man who was being raised up by God to be a mighty deliverer.

The Israelites had done evil again in the sight of God after having promised God that once they entered into the Promised land they would not forget the Lord who had delivered them out of a slave camp. Yet, in their prosperity and riches they did forget God and began doing evil in the sight of Him worshiping many false idols. God handed them over to an evil man, Cushan-Rishathaim, and they became afraid and cried out to the Lord. They said, "Help Father, I'm Afraid. We need a deliverer we are oppressed."

It is sad how we can get comfortable in our wealth and riches and then forget it was God who gives the wealth. This is what had happened to the Israelites.

It is very sad that when we are comfortable in our wealth and then lose it all, we become afraid and say, "Help Father."

He loves us and He hears us every time. It's just like children sometimes. They grow up and forget their parents. They don't call, because they are too busy, and then, when they need something, they call up and say, "Hey, dad."

Meanwhile, on the other side of town, Othniel was growing up to be a man of God. Little did he know that the Israelites were crying out for a deliverer and were afraid. Othniel grew up and was a strong man of God. God had a mighty plan for Othniel.

Othniel was to become their deliverer and deliver the Israelites from Cushan-Rishathaim. Neither the Israelites, nor Othniel really knew what was going on with the other!

God is long-suffering and loving toward His very own children. The Israelites had sinned, gone wrong, and yet God heard them.

God hears you also. You may think that you have done so wrong, that God can not hear you.

During the time in my life when I was so afraid of losing it all, I didn't think God would hear me, because I felt my sin of fear was un-forgivable. God loves His children, and hears them, no matter what. I didn't have to be oppressed and neither do you. Let all oppression be gone in your life in the name of Jesus. God is your deliverer today.

God has a plan for your life. You need to follow that plan, and listen to what He is telling you to do, and continue to walk in His ways. You could be used mightily by God, without even knowing at the moment what His plan is for your life.

When I went to meet my dad at the prison, I went because God had told me that I needed to forgive him before I could continue doing full-time missions. I had no idea that God would use me later to minister to prisoners, write books, and so much more. People write me even today to tell me of how much the reconciliation of my dad and I meant to them. I don't even know these people!

As you grow in the Lord, God wants to use you mightily for His kingdom. One can not be used mightily for the Kingdom, if one is focused on fear. You must move forward in spite of your fear.

Fear keeps you from doing God's will. Fear is a loud, roaring lion and it wants to devour you. Fear tries to silence the still small voice inside of you. God's voice is the loving, kind and gentle voice that is calling out to you today.

God wants us to be fearless and not fearful so that He can use us wherever He wants to send us. Whether it be to a prison, or to a palace to become King, God wants to use us for His Kingdom purpose. We can not be used if we are focused on fear. We can only be used if we have the fear of the Lord in our life, and God can make us fearless.

With a fearless mentality we can go anywhere, anytime, without notice from God. We can be in America one day and on the mission field in Mongolia the next day when we have a *fearless fallacy*. We can be losing it all one day and writing a book the next day when we allow the *fearless fortress* to lead us.

We can be an Othniel of life with a fearless mentality and become a person that empowers and helps deliver others from fear and oppression.

Your deliverer is here and His name is Jesus. He wants to deliver you from every single thing you are afraid of in your life so that you can have peace for the rest of your life. He longs to deliver you from your burdens so that you can stand tall and live the life He has for you. He wants to be your deliverer and deliver you from whatever it is that is troubling you today.

Othniel is dead now. He has no idea at all that we are reading about him. He had no idea he'd be famous in the kingdom of God for remaining obedient to the call upon his life.

Stay strong in God like Othniel, because that is priceless, and someone may just write about you one day.

Questions:

1. Who do you relate to in the above passage, the Israelites, or Othniel?
2. Do you want all fear in your life gone?
3. Who can you have pray with you to help you become delivered from fear?
4. When can you have this person pray with you?
5. What five things are you afraid of?

Quiet Time:

Talk to God about the many things you are afraid of. Ask Him to bring you a mentor or a prayer partner, someone you can trust.

Now, turn those five fearful things into a positive statement. For example if you are afraid of flying, you can turn that around by saying, "If God wants me to fly overseas to do a missions trip, I will not fear, I will be fearless, and with the Lord's help, focus on what it is He wants me to do in this life because He is my creator. I let go of the fear of flying, so that He can use me the way He wants to use me."

Day 8

Fear of Never Getting Married

Ruth 3:11 and now, my daughter, don't be afraid. I will do for you all you ask. All my fellow townsmen know that you are a woman of noble character.

Ruth is a woman of noble character and God is interested in our character.

Her husband had died and so had her mother in law's husband at about the same time. They had moved to another town and she was a stranger in a strange land. She worked hard several hours a day gleaning in a field. I am convinced gleaning, back in those days, was no walk in the park. I am sure she didn't have a water bottle with her, she wasn't wearing a tank top, shorts, and flip flops. She had no i-pod to keep her company while she gleaned. Her head was probably covered, and who knows how long she went without food and drink.

In the above scripture, Boaz, the kinsman-redeemer is speaking to Ruth. Apparently, all the people in town had been talking about this wonderful new woman who had come to town and how hard she worked.

This man Boaz was very wealthy and ends up marrying Ruth.

Little did Ruth know that the townsmen had been watching her and reporting back to Boaz what they noticed in Ruth. She was just being a diligent, hard working woman, doing her daily routine. The scriptures don't say whether Ruth liked it or not, she had actually decided long ago, that she would go wherever her mother in law went. Ruth was true to her word and Ruth's noble character was spread to Boaz.

When Ruth's husband died, she had no idea that many years later God would give her more than she had before. Ruth simply submitted to God's plan for her life.

This helped me in the area of fear, especially the fear of never getting married, because of God's ultimate control of our lives. God knew Boaz long before Ruth did and God had been making a way for this to happen all along.

When you read the Old Testament, you can follow it word for word up to this event in history and it spells it out completely how these two meet and how they end up becoming a couple in the genealogy of Jesus Christ!

Ruth was a poor Moabite widow gleaning in a field. No one expected Boaz, the wealthiest man around to take notice of her. God can bring you your husband no matter where you are. Whatever it is you do on a daily basis do it all as unto the Lord just as Ruth did and God will bless you.

God is wealthier than Boaz. God desires to be your redeemer and redeem your widow-like situation and turn it around into something so beautiful that the whole town will talk.

Don't worry about tomorrow. God's got it all figured out, and He is preparing a place for you. It is better than you can fathom. Remember too that people watch your life. People not only watch, but they talk. I wonder if the townsmen had said to Boaz, "That Ruth, she is nothing but a slacker," what Boaz would have done.

Live your life before God, not men, work diligently, and without fear.

Questions:

1. Do you have a grievance against your mother-in-law?
2. Do you have a grievance against anyone?
3. Are you doing your work daily as unto God?
4. Do you work hard like Ruth did day in and day out, no matter what?
5. Do you look for ways to please your boss all for the glory of God?
6. Do you glean with a good attitude, even when you don't get your way?

Quiet time:

Talk to God about the grievances you have towards others. Share with Him how you feel you have been hurt or mis-treated. Give the results to the Lord. Ask Him to help you not take matters into your own hands.

Write down the grievances you have had towards others. Ask God to forgive you, because He can not bless you if you are angry at your mother-in-law, spouse or boss. Forgive them and ask yourself what it is that needs to be let go in re-gards to them.

Ask God to help you to not worry about anything. Fear and worry can not co-exist with peace. If you are worried, write down what you are worried about, for example write out, "I am worried about how to pay the mortgage this month." As God to give you a worry free life in regards to the area of money, and ask Him to take control of your finances.

Day 9

Fear of Not Getting Pregnant

1 Samuel 1:17 Eli answered, "Go in peace, and may the God of Israel grant you what you have asked of him."

Year after year, Hannah longed for a son. She would spend hours in the temple crying out to God for this request. The scriptures actually say that Hannah was bitter of soul, in anguish, and wept and prayed! Eli the priest had been watching her the whole time, and she was so caught up in her praying, she had no idea she was being watched. Eli actually accused her of being drunk and she exclaimed that she was crying out to the Lord. Hannah did not tell Eli what she was praying.

Peace is apparently a big thing to God. After Eli told her to go in peace, Hannah did, and she conceived and gave birth to a son and he was dedicated to God.
Eli the prophet had told Hannah to go in peace, because she had been a prayer warrior and sought God for a child daily. Eli also told her that God would grant her request.

What is a grant in our culture today? A grant is a large sum of money given to one in need. Perhaps that grant is for college or to build a non-profit organization. Whatever the grant is for it is given only after much paperwork is filled out and approved.

Hannah had been given a grant by God because of her faithful prayers. Hannah did not have to fill out any paperwork, nor did Hannah have to get approved. She only had to cry out to her Father, 'Help Father, I'm afraid I will have no children.' She was already approved by God. You are approved by God today.

Why are you crying? What has you in despair? What is it that you so desperately want, need, or desire? It is ok if you are in anguish, grief, or even despair. Be diligent in your prayers and don't stop praying! Hannah prayed year after year!

Know that God hears you and He will answer. It may not be in your time table, but it will be in His.

Hannah prayed in the midst of her anguish and she gave her anguish to God. Hannah left the church in peace. Go to God, and tell Him you are in anguish today, then let it go at the altar. God will take your grief and grant you peace.

Samuel is a great book of the bible because Samuel is used greatly by God, and I am convinced that it is because of a mother's diligent love for her son, and for her prayers.

There are times in our lives when we all cry and long for something that is extremely urgent to us. God hears you. God knows and is aware of the sense of urgency in your prayers.

God hears the siren like sounds in your voice. He sees the red light flashing around and around in your emergency prayers and knows this is urgent for you.

This passage is a beautiful one and can help us all in our anguish and grief. God desires us all to have peace and that He will grant us our requests as long as they are in His will.

God heard the cries of Hannah's heart and she gave birth to a son and named him Samuel. Samuel ended up being used as a prayer warrior just like his mother Hannah had been a prayer warrior!

Hannah did not stay consumed with her fear. She took the advice of the priest and received the grant of the peace of God in her life and that, my friend, is when she became pregnant. After she let go of her sobbing, God granted her peace and a baby.

Let go of your sobbing. Keep on praying. Don't give up! Your request has been answered. Your peace has been granted. You are approved.

Questions:

1. Are you going about your life sobbing in your soul?
2. What do you long for?
3. I am here to act on behalf of that priest! I say to you, let go of your sobbing, and go about your life in peace. Write out what you are crying in your heart to the Lord for, whether it be a job promotion, a new car, or a good marriage. Write it out, and then turn your sobbing into peace and watch God answer that prayer in His time.
4. Whatever it is you have just written out, dedicate it to the Lord. Tell the Lord that if you get that promotion, it will be used for His glory and purpose. Tell Him that if you get a peaceful marriage, your marriage will be dedicated to Him all the days of your life. Give back to God what it is you so long for.
5. What do you need granted to you?

Quiet time:

Share with God the grant you need today. Talk to Him about what it is you long for in your heart. Cry out to Him about this and then let it go and leave the results to God.

Write this out on a piece of paper, "I, your Father, have granted, (your request)." Date it for today's date. Watch God answer.

Day 10

Fear of Not Having a Home

2 Samuel 7:9-11 I have been with you wherever you have gone and I have cut off all your enemies from before you. Now I will make your name great, like the names of the greatest men of the earth. And I will provide a place for my people Israel and will plant them so that they can have a home of their own and no longer be disturbed. Wicked people will not oppress them anymore, as they did at the beginning and have done ever since the time I appointed leaders over my people Israel. I will also give you rest from your enemies. "The Lord declares to you that the Lord himself will establish a house for you:"

I thought many times as a child I would be homeless one day. We grew up on the Southside of town in Alabama, living in apartments, and continuously in poverty. It was challenging to think about what I wanted to be when I grew up.

Many years later, at the age of 37, I met my husband David. David is a builder. A few months after we met, I bought one of his lots and he built me a house. I lived in it for one year by myself, until the day we got married. The very thing I thought of, being homeless, God redeemed it and gave me a builder!

I remember sitting on my deck one day looking at the beautiful view crying out to God. I was listening to some worship music for a while and then suddenly it came in my spirit, "God, You knew where I would live!"

I never had to be afraid of being homeless!

I watched my husband for months put his time, blood, sweat, money and tears into my house. I watched him hire workers, work until midnight to get things done, and travel all over the place to get things for the house. I watched the lumber being put together and I watched each light bulb be put in. The lumber came from the ground that God created! Electricity came from a mere man that God created and is an all-powerful source that we can't live without today. God is more powerful than electricity. God is all-powerful, all-knowing, all-loving, and everything on earth and in the earth belongs to God.

Since my husband is a general contractor, I can give you an overview of what they are responsible for, and do.

A general contractor is a person that contracts with another person or organization to build a residential or commercial property. The contractor is the signor, and the one responsible for the means and methods to be used in the construction execution of the project in accordance with the contract documents. Said documents could include the construction agreement, budget, general, special conditions and plans for the project. The contractor is also responsible for supplying material, labor, equipment and services.

God is your contractor! God wants to build you a residential property and budget is not a concern. God is responsible for the means and methods to be used to get this construction executed. God has the plans, agreement, and special conditions already in place for you.

There is another type of builder called the Interactive Scenario Builder. This has nothing to do with a general contractor. This type of builder is a modeling and simulation, three dimensional application which was developed by Advanced Tactical Environmental Simulation Team! This team aids in the understanding of radio frequency.

God understands your frequency. If you believe in the three dimensional Father, Son and Holy Spirit, you can have rest knowing without a doubt that God understands your frequency. Your husband, your wife, your mom, your dad, your sibling or coworker may not understand your frequency, but God does.

God is building something beautiful in your life. He takes great care, concern and planning to give you the best. God is traveling from place to place looking for the perfect lighting for the favorite room of your house.

God is the light! Your heart is His home.

It is not God's plan for you to live a life of being disturbed, scared, and homeless. It is God's plan for your life to have a life of safety, peace, security, and rest from your enemies. However, we must choose to pray continuously, be real before God, for He knows it all anyway. He knows your heart, and He wants you to diligently seek Him for your life. As you do this He will be making a place for you on this earth and it will be a wonderful place just for you.

Questions:

1. What does your dream house look like?
2. Who is building your life?
3. Do you diligently seek Him or do you give up after a few prayers?
4. How is your frequency today?
5. Have you ever considered that everything belongs to God and not you?
6. Do you really believe that everything on earth under heaven belongs to God?
7. Is that belief a head knowledge or heart knowledge?
8. How can that belief become embedded in your character, that everything belongs to God and not you?

Quiet Time:

Write out a blueprint of your ideal life. Write out what it would look like. Write out the meaning of your life. Write out what it would be, who would share it with you, if you could build your perfect life.

Now ask God to build your perfect life. Ask God to build your dream life, and to help you delight in the Lord as the builder of your life. Tell Him your dreams, and show God your blueprint. Dedicate the dreams and the blueprint to the Lord. Ask the builder of your life to build for you. Ask the builder of your life to give you the blueprint He wants you to have, and to receive. Submit your blueprint, and your dreams to the builder.

Day 11

Fear of not being Safe

1 Kings 4:24 & 25 "For he ruled over all the kingdoms west of the River, from Tiphsah to Gaza, and had peace on all sides. During Solomon's lifetime Judah and Israel, from Dan to Beersheba, lived in safety, each man under his own fig tree."

Wh
hat does the word safe mean to you? What does safety look like to you?

In Webster's Dictionary, this is what safety means:

1. The condition or state of being safe; freedom from danger or hazard; exemption from hurt, injury, or loss.

2. Freedom from whatever exposes one to danger or from liability to cause danger or harm; safeness; hence, the quality of making safe or secure, or of giving confidence, justifying trust, insuring against harm or loss, etc.

3. Preservation from escape; close custody.

In the Strong's concordance the word safety in the above passage means:

In Hebrew the word is batach which means

1. A place of refuge

2. Both the fact (security) and the feeling (trust).

3. Assurance, Boldly, Confident, Secure, Sure, and Hope.

In Greek the word is blaberos which means

1. From injury, from hurt

King Solomon was King David's son. One time Solomon had a dream and God asked Solomon whatever it was he desired he would give it to Solomon. Solomon asked for wisdom to be able to discern what was best for the people he was leading. God gave Solomon his request, along with a long life, riches, and more. Solomon was one of the greatest rulers that ever lived. Because of his request to God the people ended up living in safety after having had years of fighting, fear and calamity.

It seemed important enough to God for the people to live in safety. Because of Solomon's request to the Lord, God granted the people safety. Solomon's request for wisdom to lead the people was out of his sincere heart for God and for people. His request was also out of a place where he was going to be doing God's will, leading the people, and Solomon asked for wisdom to lead those people. Solomon was in the center of God's will and asked God in accordance to God's plan for his life.

We can not manipulate God into giving us what we want. We can not say, "I want riches so I am going to pray for wisdom, like Solomon did and maybe God will give them to me." God is all about our hearts more than concerned with what it is we want. God loves people and so did Solomon and out of that care and concern for others God granted Solomon not only wisdom, but more. In the end the people of that day lived in safety for many years because of Solomon's heart.

What does your heart look like? I know in my own life at times that my heart has not been right before God and I have prayed selfish prayers to get what I want. God knows all of this. It is God's best interest to change our hearts, to make it more like His, so that He will love to bless us and give us even more than we ask. In the end, He desires not only to bless us but to use us to bless others!

God desires you to be free from fear and live in a place of trust, peace, and safety. Ask God to help you to change your heart to become more and more like His just because of who He is. Then watch Him turn your life into a place of utmost safety. Your safety is important to your loving Father God.

Questions:

1. What does safety look like to you?
2. What does your heart look like?
3. What is security to you?
4. Have you tried to manipulate God?

Quiet Time:

Write a letter to God, asking Him for wisdom. Tell Him what it is you need wisdom for. It could be in your marriage, your job, etc, but that you want that wisdom to be something for the other person, not yourself. You want wisdom so that you can be a blessing to your job, and to your spouse. Ask God to help you let go of any animosity that you have against those at work, or in your marriage

Tell God honestly what it is that you need most right now, whether it be safety, security, peace or whatever. Ask Him to help you to receive that in your heart so that you can be a blessing to others.

Tell God that you want to be a bold person, secure in Him, and confident

Day 12

Fear of not being Healed

2 Kings 20:5 "Go back and tell King Hezekiah, the leader of my people, "This is what the Lord, the God of your father David, says" I have heard your prayer and seen your tears; I will heal you. On the third day from now you will go up to the temple of the Lord."

K ing Hezekiah was the 11th generation in the line of King Solomon, who was King David's son. What does this mean? King Hezekiah was King Solomon's great, great, great, great, great (well, you get the idea) grandson!

King Hezekiah had been ill to the point of death. God sent the prophet Isaiah to him to tell him to get his house in order, because Hezekiah was going to die. Hezekiah prays to the Lord and that changes his destiny.

This is Hezekiah's prayer recorded in 2 Kings 20: 2-3 *Hezekiah turned his face to the wall and prayed to the Lord, "Remember, o Lord, how I have walked before you faithfully and with wholehearted devotion and have done what is good in your eyes." And Hezekiah wept bitterly.*

That's it. No long lengthy prayer and putting on sackcloth and ashes. He just turned to the wall, and prayed a little prayer. Then, Hezekiah wept, and wept bitterly! Hezekiah was not ready to die.

Hezekiah had hit a wall in his life-a wall of death! Death was staring him right in the face and Hezekiah chose to fight death with prayer. The walls of death fell down and Hezekiah lived-fifteen more years!

You may have hit a wall in your life. You may have hit a wall of debt, a wall of despair, a wall of sickness, a wall of poverty, a wall of troubled relationships-whatever is your wall God wants that wall in your life to come tumbling down. You need to pray fervently. You need to have a victory in your life today and God wants to give you that victory!

I wonder if those tears of weeping bitterly were of bitter soul. I wonder if Hezekiah was having some regrets about his life. I wonder if Hezekiah was crying those gut-wrenching tears in the hopes to have a second chance at life. I doubt Hezekiah was having a pity-party. Tears of sadness are cleansing-God uses tears to heal us. Don't cry poor me, but cry out to the One who is able to give you victory.

If you knew you were about to die, and given a second chance, how would you live?

Not only does his prayer change his life, but it changed my life as well.

God wants to give you a second chance!

God wants to heal our disease. God wants to heal us of all our iniquities. He does not want us to die in the situation we are in, filled with anger, fear, strife, or sickness. Anger, fear, and strife are all sicknesses that God wants to heal. God wants us to live a long, productive life and to do His will on this earth.

Hezekiah ends up building a pool, and a tunnel in which he used it to help others and bring them clean water. Hezekiah is also one of the men in the lineage of Jesus that you can read about in the book of Matthew.

The pool that Hezekiah built represented a spiritual pool of healing in the Kingdom of God. Hezekiah had been ill to the point of death and now he was swimming for the Kingdom of God!

Are you ill today? Do you feel as though you are ill to the point of death? Maybe you are ill to the point of death in the area of your finances, marriage, or relationships with others. If so, Hezekiah's prayer is for you. If you have been faithful to the Lord, you can remind God of your service to Him. You can also weep bitterly if you need to, and tell God that you are not ready to lose your home, lose your job, lose your loved one. God hears you. God will answer your prayer. God does not want to bring death, God wants to bring life. Whatever it is that you feel you are losing today, perhaps it may be that you feel you are losing your mere sanity, talk to God about that.

Remove all distractions from your life. I believe Hezekiah turning to the wall to pray was so that he could fully focus on God, and God alone. I believe he was in deep pain, and needed to talk to God in his very own prayer closet, and cry out deeply to His creator, His Father. I also believe that Hezekiah was making a stand, facing the wall, which was his sickness. He was facing it head on and not denying it was there. He was turning his face toward the sickness, facing the heat, and saying, "Help Lord heal me!"

Get to your prayer closet. Get to a quiet place where you can cry out to the Lord about your illness, whatever that illness may be. There are many illnesses we face and those illnesses are not just physical.

God is building you a swimming pool. Maybe that pool will be used to bring people clean water, or maybe God will send you to Mongolia to help the orphans, like me.

Or maybe, just maybe, the living Water will pour out so much water in your life, that you will be completely healed and refreshed today.

God wants your fear healed. He does not want you dying with fear in your life. He wants you set free from all fear so that you can be a blessing. He wants you to be set free and delivered from fear so that your life is not a waste. He desires you to take a dive into the deep, and that means diving into the pool of pure, healing waters. He wants to deep things for you, by the healing pool.

Questions:

1. Are you afraid of dying?
2. Do you have distractions in your life that keep you from doing God's will?
3. What are those distractions?
4. Are you "ill" today?
5. What are your ailments? (Physically, spiritually, emotionally?)

<u>Quiet Time:</u>

Turn something shallow that is in your life into something deep.
For example: Shallow could be a negative attitude towards someone that is in your life, and God wants that attitude to be turned into something positive. Write out in your journal, the negative attitude, confess it, move on, and then turn it around into the positive.

Pray the same prayer that Hezekiah prayed, but with truth and conviction. IF you have not walked with God with wholehearted devotion, ask for His forgiveness, and then ask Him to help you walk with whole hearted devotion. Ask God to show you if you have done what is good in His eyes, or if you have done what is not good in His eyes.

Take a dive into the deep end of your life. Do one thing this week that would be deep for you. It could be something as little as listening to a friend who is in need without interruption, or it could be something big like taking that first step to confronting someone that you have needed to confront for a long time now. Take one step towards the deep end of your life, pray about it first, and then act.

Day 13

Fear of no Peace and Quiet

1 Chronicles 4:40 They found rich, good pasture and the land was spacious, peaceful and quiet. Some Hamites had lived there formerly.

God calls you His sheep. He leads his sheep to a rich, spacious, peaceful pasture.

It is not in His will for us to be in a pasture surrounded by the dingle-berries of life.

Who are 'they' in the above passage? They are Simeon's descendants. Who the heck is Simeon, you ask? Simeon is Leah's son. Who the heck is Leah? Leah is Jacob's unloved wife. You can read about the whole family for yourself in the book of Genesis.

It inspired me to think about the fact that in the scriptures we read that God saw that Leah, Jacob's wife was unloved. Jacob had worked seven years for her sister, Rachel, but Rachel's dad deceived Jacob, and gave him Leah instead. Jacob worked another seven years for Rachel. Jacob had two wives, Leah was unloved, and Rachel was loved. God had mercy on Leah, and opened up her womb, and she had more children than Rachel did. Simeon was one of them.

Simeon's descendants ended up living in places of peace, quiet, and a spacious land. Leah had not any idea of this, because by the time all this took place, Leah was dead.

Simeon and his descendants were loved by the Lord, because Leah was unloved by her husband.

God sees your pain. Maybe because of your fear, you are feeling unloved by God. Maybe you are unloved by your husband. Maybe you are unloved in general by people. If you are unloved God has a special place in His heart for you.

God loves you. It is for your sake and the sake of your descendants that He desires to give you a land with plenty of space to run, jump and shout for joy. He wants to give you a place of peace, not fear, so that you can have peace in your life. He wants to give you a quiet place, inner quiet, so that you can have serenity at all times.

This place of space, peace and quiet begins within. It takes some work, and time to get to a place of total and complete serenity. One can not have an internal quiet, with all the noise of the soul that is so loud.

You can have serenity with the help of your Father God.

He desires to give you first and foremost peace in your inmost being and out of that will flow the rest of your life, for your sake, and your descendants sake.

Questions:

1. Do you feel unloved?
2. Who do you feel doesn't love you?
3. Are you angry with them for not loving you?
4. Do you need them to love you?
5. Do you have any resentment, bitterness, or unforgiveness towards the person or people that don't love you?
6. Do you want a spacious, quiet, peaceful life?
7. Have you ever pondered for a while the fact that you are His sheep and the Shepherd leads you to still quiet calm waters?
8. Does your soul, your internal being, live in quiet waters?

<u>Quiet Time:</u>

Cry out to the Lord in regards to this situation, circumstances, and person *or* people that don't love you. Talk to him about the fact that you are unloved. Tell God that you want to be loved by them.

Ask God to forgive you for your un-forgiveness and to heal you from it. Tell God to cleanse you from all unrighteousness and ask Him to help you have whole heartedness towards Him.

Whatever it is that is noisy in your life, get it out. Get it out of your life, permanently. What I mean by that is, if a friend is too loud, too negative, too abrupt, too much for you, get them out of your life with love, but don't hang out with them so much anymore. If you watch too much TV, turn it off, and listen to some peaceful music and read a book. Do whatever you need to do. Take one step this week towards getting the loudness out of your life.

Ask the Shepherd to lead your soul to peaceful pastures.

Day 14

Fear of having no Purpose

2 Chronicles 2: 11 Hiram king of Tyre replied by letter to Solomon"
"Because the Lord loves his people, he has made you their king."

God loves you, I can't say it enough. God loves you because of who He is, not because of who we are. God's love is unconditional and eternal. God's love isn't about us. God's love for us is about Him.

Loren Cunningham, founder of Youth with a Mission was a young man sitting in Hawaii on the beach looking at the ocean, and God gave him a vision. God gave this man a vision of young people on the waves, and God told him that God would use Loren in young people's lives, so that they could go into the entire world to spread the gospel.

Little Laura Ann told her mother when she grew up she would be a missionary (this was of course after my homeless thought.) When I was 30 my sister in law told me about Ywam.

One man's choice, Loren Cunningham's to obey God, changed the course of my life, and the course of history, and many other people's lives. He did not know his act of obedience would change many people's lives, nor did he know who his life would impact. He did not even know me when I applied to Ywam!

I had the privilege of traveling from Hawaii, to Mongolia, to Fiji, to India, to China to Thailand.

Loren built a missionary base in Hawaii. When I was about 32 years old, I traveled to Hawaii to get trained to go to India. When I landed in Hawaii, the smell of beautiful plumeria was all around me, and the trees were filled with beautiful flowers, and it was February. I had been living in New Hampshire for years where it was cold in February.

I had been dating a man for many years that didn't believe in buying a woman flowers, because he said it was a waste of money. When I landed in Hawaii, I had the smell of flowers all around me! I had died and gone to a heavenly place filled with flowers that surrounded me.

God redeemed my flower drama, and little did Loren Cunningham know when he was building that missionary base, how that one act of obedience would change the course of my life, and how God would use those plumeria trees to bring about the goodness of the Lord in my heart. I also got to travel to India which was a life long dream for me.

King Solomon was building a temple for the Lord, and had sent word to the King of Tyre in regards to it. King Tyre responds to Solomon that because of God's love, He made Solomon King. It was not because of any righteous act in part of Solomon, although Solomon loved the Lord, it was because of God's love for his people.

Because the Lord loves you, He is doing something marvelous in your life. He is doing something miraculous in your life. He is making you the queen or king of something so spectacular that people all around you will say, "God did that in their life."

When God told Loren Cunningham to build a missionary base, it was because of His love for many around the world.

God loves you, and is building your life for you and for others

What is God doing in your life? The choices you make today, will lead you to the destination of tomorrow. Allow God to work out His plan in your life, and you will be amazed at what He does, and how He does it. Your name could become known throughout the world, and God's love will be spread because of you.

Do not be afraid, God is doing something wonderful in your life.

Questions:

1. Would you like to be the one person to change the course and direction for someone else's life for the better?
2. What step could you make this week towards helping another person in your life, for the better? It could be a phone call, a hug, or taking someone out for coffee.
3. Would you like to be used so miraculously that one decision you make helps to bring the salvation of many people?
4. Would you like the Lord to use you for His purpose, not your purpose?
5. Are you willing to do whatever it takes to allow God to use you for His purpose?

Quiet Time:

Tell God thanks for the people that have made a difference in your life, and ask God to use you.

Is there someone in your life that their choice has changed your life, if so, write them a letter thanking them for what a difference they have made in your life, and how their one action changed your life, and inspired you.

Day 15

Fear of God's Hand not being on Your Life

Ezra 7:27 & 28 Praise be to the Lord, the God of our fathers, who has put it into the king's heart to bring honor to the house of the Lord in Jerusalem in this way and who has extended his good favor to me before the king and his advisers and all the king's powerful officials. Because of the hand of the Lord my God was on me, I took courage and gathered leading men from Israel to go up with me.

The journey of your life could have been through more valleys than peaks. The journey of your life could have led you from living a life in the street, to living a life in a prison. The journey of your life could have been down dark, dreary paths that led to a shack at the end of the road. The journey of your life could have been through more poverty than prosperity. The journey of your life could have been through a mountain ravine in the middle of a desert, without clean water when you were thirsty. The journey of your life could have been mostly uphill both ways in the snow without snow boots.

The past does not have to dictate your future! Put your hand in the hand of the man who stilled the water. Put your hand in the hand of the man who calmed the sea. Put your hand in the hand of the one who is your creator, He will lead you to go up, to a better life with a better view!

What has your journey been? Would your life look differently if you knew for certain that God's hand was on you, and you were being highly regarded by a King?

God had been setting Ezra up for years for his task at hand. Ezra had studied the word of God for many years, and was dedicated to teaching others about it. God's hand was on Ezra from child hood, and God had a plan to use Ezra. The scriptures tell us that the gracious hand of God was upon him, and that was because Ezra had devoted himself to the things of the Lord. Ezra was on a mission, and he was focused to complete it.

Meanwhile, over in Jerusalem, the Israelites were there, not knowing about Ezra coming up from out of nowhere to help them and guide them. The Israelites had married foreign women, against God's command, and their lives were not in the best condition because of their sin.

On the other side of town, God was raising Ezra up, who had been studying the scriptures for many, many years, and it was his call upon his life to go to Jerusalem and help the troubled Israelites.

Ezra had obviously become a little fearful of the journey ahead, because the scriptures tell us that Ezra took courage, realizing that God's hand was upon him.

Ezra took courage from the gracious hand of God Himself, who desires to give courage graciously to us all.

In Hebrew the word hand means: Yad, *Indicating power, direction, able, about, armholes, at, axletree, because of, beside, border, bounty, broad, handed by charge, coast, consecrate, creditor, custody, debt, dominion, enough, fellowship, force, labor, large, ledge, mine, ministry, near, order, ordinance, our, parts, pain, power, presumptuous, service, side, sore, state, stay draw with strength.* In Greek it is Lepsis, means: *Robber, thief!* No, I am not kidding, you can look it up in the Strong's concordance.

No, God is not a Robber.

I have been in a bank robbery, held at gunpoint. I have seen how fast a robber can move, and under 60 seconds, their hand can quickly take the money out of our drawers. When the police came for each of us to give our statement, none of us mentioned the time it took for the robber to take our cash. However, it was the police officer who explained to us how quickly the bank robber got out of that bank with the cash!

In the scriptures previously, they state that it only took five months for Ezra to make a journey to the King to get that letter from him. Ezra came a long way, on foot, to get that letter. The scriptures also tell us that the gracious hand of the Lord God was on him. This means God accelerated time for Ezra to get that letter so that Ezra could quickly get to the Israelites to help them out with their current problem. Not only did God accelerate time for Ezra, God also quickly, efficiently, and speedily gives graciously to all who ask of Him, as quick as a bank robber can steal cash from a teller!

The Israelites probably felt like it was a long time while they were waiting at-least ten months, on something to happen for them. They had not any idea of Ezra's coming. It is not like Ezra could shoot them an email, a text message, or make a phone call to tell them he was on their way, just hang on! He also couldn't take a quick plane ride. He had to travel to the King first, and then to the Israelites, ON FOOT!

Yet speedy God showed up, and accelerated time for Ezra. Now only a few months later, Ezra was on his way to help out the Israelites with their problem.

Ezra showed up just in time to help them, and he showed up with treasures from the King himself. King Artaxerxes had given Ezra silver and gold, helpers and wheat, wine, olive oil, and salt without limit! The King mentions to Ezra also in his agreement that he sees how much wisdom Ezra has, and he can do whatever he wishes upon his arrival in Jerusalem, in accordance to God.

The King also decrees that whoever does not obey Ezra must be punished by death, banishment, confiscation of property or imprisonment!

You can read about this decree in the book of Ezra chapter 7.

Whatever is going on in your life, remain close to God during this difficult time. God will move people's hearts on account of you, His name will be praised, and you will be talked about all over town because of your great diligence to God. Not only that, you could be noticed by a King.

By the way, you already are, His name is King Jesus!

Questions:

1. What do you need from God, right now, quickly?(the key word is quickly)
2. If you were God, and you had something to say to you, what would you say?
3. If you were God, and you had something to give to you right now, what would you give?

Quiet Time:

Take both of your hands, and open them up, and look at them for a while. Now close your eyes, and pray to the Lord. Ask God to speak to you about His hand. Picture His hand wiping every tear from your eye, and giving you graciously whatever it is you need. Write in your journal what God gives to you, graciously. Picture His blood coming over you, graciously and cleansing you.

Open your hand up to someone graciously this week. Maybe you are supposed to buy someone flowers, or maybe you are supposed to introduce yourself to a stranger and shake their hand. Whatever it is, open up your hand as gratefulness to God for Him extending His hand to you.

Write down on a piece of paper what you want to give God this week. Put that piece of paper somewhere for you to remind yourself that you are giving that to God. It does not have to be money. Extend your hand to God.

Make a list of what your hands have done lately. If you have pushed the lawn mower, write it down. If you have washed dishes, write it down. If you have made the bed, write it down. Whatever your hands have been put to, or given, write it down.

Now, realize that God can do more than your very own hands have done! Receive from the Lord's hand!

Day 16

Fear of Losing

Nehemiah 4:14 after I looked things over, I stood up and said to the nobles, the officials and the rest of the people, "don't be afraid of them. Remember the Lord who is great and awesome, and fight for your brothers, your sons, and your daughters, your wives and your homes."

Nehemiah was a prayer warrior. He used prayer to fight his battles. Nehemiah had a burden on his heart. When he heard that the Israelites life was in shambles after the walls of Jerusalem had fallen down he became concerned and prayed. The walls of Jerusalem were at that time walls of protection, peace and safety. Now that the walls had been torn down, the Israelites peace, safety and protection were gone. Nehemiah heard about this many miles away, and became burdened with one concern, to rebuild the wall for the people. He left his place of prominence to go rebuild the wall for the Israelites. He went to the King to get permission, and before talking to the King he states that he was afraid. Nehemiah prayed first before talking to the King, and the King granted his request.

After getting permission, Nehemiah had lots of opposition to the rebuilding. In Nehemiah chapter 4 three different times Nehemiah had negative comments and threats in regards to the rebuilding. The very people that were rebuilding the people, from the house of Judah, said they were getting tired and could not rebuild. The people that were against the jews stated that they were going to kill them all. The Jews that lived near Nehemiah came to him and said that wherever Nehemiah would turn next, people would be waiting to kill him. These attacks and attitudes against Nehemiah were not deserved. Nehemiah had done nothing wrong.

I don't know about you, but at that point, I may have told all the workers to go home, they were all fired, and I would have taken a vacation to get away from the crazy people that were trying to kill me. Since I was King, I would have gone to Prague or Costa Rica, and eaten fresh fruit in peace for a while.

In the midst of the uncertainty, fear, and threats Nehemiah chose to leave his place of prominence, to humble him self, and go to a place of utter ruin. He also chose to pray.

He did not let fear become his burden. He prayed and allowed the burden bearer to help him through his mission.

Your life may be in ruins right now, yet God is doing something new in your life.

God is interested in our internal character, not our circumstances. God wants us to learn to be men and women of noble character such as Nehemiah when others may be coming against us. God is about people and cares about our internal soul more than what other people are saying against us. He wants His sons and daughters to pray without ceasing and to pray for those that persecute them. This is a hard teaching but it is one we must learn if we are going to have strong character for God.

You say, "You don't know all the people that are against me right now. You don't know how many people at work and at home have attacked me without cause verbally. You don't know the girl at work that drives me crazy and tries daily to get me fired. You don't know how mean my husband is."

No, I don't and you don't know about my situations or circumstances either. This is not a competition of who has the worst verbal attacks or unjust situations going on in their life. Nehemiah had plenty of opposition going on all around him, yet He chose to obey God, and His true character did shine through in the midst of these challenging times. He was refined in the fire and became as pure gold. Pure gold is about our internal character not about our outward circumstances.

Nehemiah travels to Jerusalem and he faced further opposition. There were two people that kept thinking lies about Nehemiah and even wrote him a letter telling him what they thought. He responded in prayer.

"Lord, strengthen my hands." Nehemiah 6:9 part B.

Nehemiah prayed, to the Lord that God would strengthen His hands! People were threatening the building of the wall and Nehemiah asked for strength in the very area that was being attacked! Nehemiah asked God to strengthen His hands to re-build!

The walls got re-built and the Israelites were in safety and peace again.

If you are being attacked today then ask God to strengthen you in the very area you are being attacked. Don't ask God to change other people. Ask God to help you through the situation. Ask God to help you re-build your life!

Maybe the walls of protection, peace and safety in your own life have been torn down, ripped apart, crushed, battered and broken. Maybe you are in a place of utter despair, depression, worry, doubt, fear, and fret. Maybe you feel very vulnerable right now, and concerned about your future. Maybe your own spiritual life has been torn down. Maybe your physical body has been torn down. I don't know what needs to be re-built but God does.

God hears your cries, as he heard the cries of the Israelites. He could be raising up a deliverer for you, or he could be raising you up. He wants to do something new in your life, so that He can get the glory. He wants to re-build something so beautiful in your life that is even better than what you had before. He wants to be the one to re-build, and He does not want you re-building your life in your own strength. He has plans for you, and He has something for you that is great. You need to continuously be in prayer and asking God during this time what it is He wants out of your life.

Jerusalem lied in ruins. God raised up Nehemiah to re-build it. If your life is currently in ruins, and you ask God what it is He wants to do with your life, He will hear you, bless you, and answer you. Not only that, but when you set out for the task that He has asked you to do, He will provide for you everything you need, and will take care of you. This is not a time for you to be doing anything in your own strength, you need the mighty hand of God on your side, and you need to act now, and act with diligence and prayer.

The plan of God for Nehemiah's life wasn't about the wall of Jerusalem, it was actually about the Israelites character and the character of Nehemiah. After the wall was re-built the Israelites confessed their sins, repented and returned to God.

The call of God on your life is about people and character.

Seek Him diligently during these days, and God will re-build your life into what He wants. It may not be what you want, but it will be better than you can do on your own.

Questions:

1. What area of your life do you need strength in right now?
2. What is ruined in your life?
3. What needs re-building?
4. Have you been threatened lately
5. Is your job being threatened, is your marriage threatened, is your friendship with someone threatened?

<u>Quiet Time:</u>

Make one goal this week to begin rebuilding your life. If you need your internal heart rebuilt because it is broken, take one step towards that this week for more healing. It may be that you need to contact a Pastor and meet with them once a week for prayer. It may be that you need your marriage rebuilt, if that is the case, find a married couple that you trust, and ask them for prayer, and to give you some Godly advice about your marriage. Or something simple could be that your bedroom is trashed, and you need to clean it. Do something this week to rebuild your life, and bring order to your life

Do not run away from the situation, and do not react. Wait upon the Lord, so He can renew your strength in this area.

Take a long walk this week in a serene place, and ask God if you are in ruins internally. Ask Him to be your guide. Recommit your plans to the Lord, and you will succeed.

Write out Nehemiah's prayer and put it somewhere for you to see, permanently 'Lord, strengthen my _____' and you fill in the blank with whatever it is that you need strength for. Put the prayer on your frig, in your car, or wherever you are most, so that prayer can become a part of your inmost being.

Day 17

Fear of Facing God

Esther 5:2 "When he saw Queen Esther standing in the court, he was pleased with her and held out to her the gold scepter that was in his hand. So Esther approached and touched the tip of the scepter."

Esther 8:6 "For how can I bear to see disaster fall on my people? How can I bear to see the destruction of my family?"

Once upon a time in a land near the citadel of Susa, there lived a beautiful young girl named Hadassah. She was known in her region as Esther, but her birth name was Hadassah. She was very young when her parents died. She was then adopted by her Uncle Mordecai. Mordecai was actually Hadassah's cousin, yet Mordecai raised her as his own.

Esther was a Jewish girl and had been forbidden by her Uncle to tell anyone about her nationality. The bible tells us that Esther had been obedient to her Uncle ever since he adopted her. (Esther chapter 2:20). This is extremely important as you read further.

King Xerxes first Queen was Vashti. The bible tells us that the King wanted Queen Vashti to come out to a banquet he was having because she was very beautiful. Queen Vashti refused to do this and no one could understand why she refused the King's orders. The King became angry because the Queen refused his orders. He sought out counsel and the counsel told him to take the crown away from Vashti because if all the other women of the town find out about this then they wouldn't respect or obey their husbands and there would be discord.

The King took the crown away and began looking for another queen. Esther won his favor and he made her Queen.

In contemplating the book of Esther you can discover several things about Esther's character.

The book of Esther starts out by explaining to us the fact that Queen Vashti refused her husband's orders. This infuriated him and he got himself another Queen. In chapter 2 we read the fine print, (if you blink you will quickly dismiss verse 20 as if it is not important), that Esther had 'obeyed' Mordecai's instructions since she was a little girl.

Apparently it is important for us, (now wives don't get angry when you read this), to obey our husbands. I know this is not a very popular subject. However, I think as Christian women it is important for us to understand that God is about obedience to our authority. Now if a husband asks us to sin then we are not to obey him. A husband is also not to use his authority to abuse women. A husband is called in scripture to love his wives as Jesus loves His church and gave Himself up for her. We are to obey our men as unto the Lord-as if we were obeying King Jesus Himself.

The King in the book of Esther was pleased with his Queen and was willing to give her his kingdom and anything she desired.

The King continuously gave his Queen what she requested. He did not use his power to try to manipulate or force his ways upon his queen. Esther knew about obedience because she had been doing it since she was little. This was part of her character. Queen Vashti, the first Queen, disobeyed the Kings orders and he gave her crown to another.

The bible is clear about Godly character and how a woman is to treat her man. If women will allow God to develop Godly character then women will win the favor of their husbands. Esther is a great book to study if you want to understand how to develop Godly character.

It is clear that God honors Esther because she approached her husband in such a way that it won his favor. Therefore she was able to release her burden and her fears to her husband and he took care of the entire situation on his wife's behalf!

I don't know about you but I'm willing to obey my husband knowing that he is a man of God and will do anything for me that is in his power if it is good for me.

God longs to give you the Kingdom and He is interested in our obedience and our character. He longs to do anything for you if it is good for you.

He holds everything in His hands and longs to give you what it is you desire. He longs for obedience and a willing heart to obey Him in all situations.

The scripture is clear, God is about obedience. Esther had been obedient since she was a child to her Uncle Mordecai and that was her character. Therefore, it is clear that once Esther became Queen she would respect and obey her husband the King.

When Esther learned that the Jewish people were about to be exterminated her heart became heavy. She knew she had to talk to her husband about this but needed to wait for the opportune time. She did not just blurt out what it was she wanted; nor did she burden him with her heavy heart. She simply pondered the matters in her heart and waited until it was appropriate for her to approach her husband and she did so with faith and a pure heart.

Esther was standing in the court after going through six months of being silent and intense beauty treatments. She was only able to enter the court at the opportune time. When she entered the court at the King's command, she had a heavy burden on her heart because of all that the Jewish people e were about to endure.

The King held out the golden scepter and she was able to approach the throne boldly. She approached it boldly, touched the tip of the scepter and without fear. She then announced her burden to the King!

Now, as a woman, it must have been challenging to wait six months to bring up this subject matter with her husband. I do not know many wives today who could wait that long to talk to their husbands about something. For Esther it wasn't about her it was about the Jewish people. She would do whatever it took to make sure that she handled this situation with Godly character. She also knew how to plead a case with her husband who was King and had the power to do what she requested. There is a way to plead a case with our husbands even today. We must learn how to approach our husbands and when. We must give them the respect they need and not trouble them with our troubles so much. If we are believers then we can go to the One who holds the keys to the Kingdom and He will be our burden bearer.

Esther had to go through a lot to get to the point of touching the tip of the golden scepter. Yet in just touching the tip of the King's scepter it was enough to grant Esther's request!

In biblical times the golden scepter represented authority. The queen could not just approach the king. She had to have permission to approach the king or she could get the death penalty. Esther knew she had a job to do for her people were going to be killed. When Mordecai asks Esther to approach the king they decided that there should be three days of fasting. On the third day, after that fasting is when Esther approached the king.

This signifies the resurrection of our Lord.

God's golden scepter is held out for you today. You can approach the throne boldly with your heavy burden that is in your heart. Maybe you have it all together on the outside but inside you have a heavy heart.

All you need to do is call on the name of King Jesus in your heart to approach the throne and touch the tip of the golden scepter.

What you see God doing in your life is just the tip of the iceberg. God has much more for you than you have today and He longs for you to receive.

The word golden in the Hebrew language:

Zahab: *To shimmer gold. Something gold colored as <u>oil.</u>*

The scepter in the Hebrew in the above scripture comes from the word:

Sharbiyt

A rod of empire

You are very precious in God's sight and to Him you are beautiful. He longs to give you His anointing oil. He holds the golden empire in His hand and He longs to pour out His anointing oil over you so that you can be all that He has called you to be. That is priceless.

Think about this; Esther approached the King's throne who was holding out this oil like rod that was extremely large. The gold was so pure on this rod that it appeared to look like oil. Esther had a heavy burden and the King was able to do for her all she requested so that her people would not be exterminated.

Whatever God wants you to do with your life, He is pouring out His anointing oil over you and longs to give you the keys to His Kingdom.

He is interested in you so much so that He says to you today to touch His golden scepter, just touch the tip of it and you will receive enough of my anointing oil to bring about the purpose that I have laid out for you. I will equip you to do the task that I have for you.

You have a calling on your life and it will not be carried out to completion until you approach the throne boldly, without fear and touch the tip of the golden scepter! Allow Him to remove your burden and pour out His oil all over you.

You don't have to prepare anything to approach the King but your heart. All you have to do is go to King Jesus and present your burden to Him in His name. You don't have to wait; you don't have to do anything but be yourself.

Perhaps God has called you to go on a mission's trip but you don't have the funds. Perhaps God has called you to be a speaker or a writer and you don't have any idea how to get published or where to do your first speaking engagement. Perhaps you are called to be a manager of a bank and you don't feel you know how to manage people. Perhaps you are afraid that someone in your family is about to go through something unbearable. Approach the throne today and receive the golden scepter that is held out for you and has enough power in His hands to give you the Kingdom. He will take care of you and all that you need and already has the answer in His hand.

You are His beautiful Bride. You can walk down the corridor, approach the throne, reach out your hand and touch the tip of the scepter. So much healing, life and abundance will come into you and pour all over you!

If an earthly King knows how to answer Esther's request, how much more does Jesus Christ want to answer yours?

He wants to give you beauty treatments, but those beauty treatments are from the inside out. He wants your heart to become beautiful for Him. He desires you to come to Him with your petitions, requests, fears and needs.

Take your rightful position, face the King boldly, and touch the tip of the golden scepter.

Questions:

1. Are you afraid of approaching God?
2. Do you feel unworthy to approach the King?
3. Have you ever considered that God's golden scepter is held out for you?
4. Are you a confident woman of God?
5. What do you think about yourself?
6. Do you believe that God holds the keys to the Kingdom and can give you whatever is good for you?
7. Do you approach the throne boldly, as Esther did?

Quiet Time:

If you can afford it, go get a manicure, pedicure, or facial treatment. If you can not afford it, save two dollars a week until you have saved up enough $ and put it in a 'beauty treatment fund.' (guys, you can have a pedicure, they are great.) While you are having your beauty treatment, talk to the King in your heart. Tell Him to clean you up inside, and to make you beautiful for Him.

If you are doing this as a group bible study then all of you need to go together and reflect on how God thinks you are beautiful and discuss it after over coffee.

Write down how you would act, look, speak, behave, and think if you were a Queen, or King. Be specific. Write:

If I were Queen or King for a day I would:

After you have written all that down, discuss it with someone, have an open conversation with another person about how they would act if they were Queen or King.

Between the two of you, pray together. Talk to God about being a Queen or King, with your friend agreeing with you in prayer.

Seal your paper up in an envelope, and label the envelope Queen_____(your name) or King _____.' Address the envelope, and mail it back to yourself. When you receive the letter back, open it up and be reminded again how a Queen or King acts.

Treat yourself to a hotel room sometime in the future, make a date with God, to be just with Him for an entire evening. If you have children, ask your spouse to keep the kids for the night while you and God have a night of beauty in that hotel room you and Him, together. Turn off the cell phone, and just listen to God for a night. Pray, fast, or do whatever it is you need to do for yourself, to have a whole entire evening reading your bible, talking to God, and just being made over by Him.

Day 18

Fear of Life being over while You are Alive

Job 42:10 "After Job had prayed for his friends, the Lord made him prosperous again and gave him twice as much as he had before."

Job was the most righteous man on the planet that ever lived and had more difficult times than almost anyone in the Bible other than Jesus or Paul.

The book of Job is not popular. However, Job is a powerful book of the Bible and has a profound message.

God is interested in our character. I can not say that enough. God is great, wonderful, awesome, and loves His kids.

The devil had been browsing around the earth, seeking for someone to devour. God asked the devil what he had been doing that day, and satan told God. God gave satan permission to do with Job what he wanted except kill him.

Job lost his children, his wealth, his health. All he had left with was his wife and some dumb friends that had no clue into what God was doing with Job's life.

Throughout the book of Job, Job has a conversation with himself, with his friends, and with God. He talks about how he had feared some things in his life, and those fears all came true.

He questions the day he was born, even curses it, and sits there in misery- scraping the boils off his body. His friends give him some stupid suggestions and advice, and have no clue that God is doing something better in Job's life than they could even imagine.

Job was a righteous man, and handled the untimely circumstances in his life by talking to God, and discussing, pondering, and praying. He shared with God what was on his heart during those difficult days of losing it all, and God heard him. God tells Job that He is in charge, and has a plan for him. God tells Job about His power, might, strength, and love. This beautiful discussion between God and Job is what God wants for our lives.

When we are losing it all, God wants us to find Him and ourselves. God wants us to focus on Him, not on the loss.

Job went through grief, and after he prayed for his friends, (the very ones that accused Job of sinning), God blessed Job's life more than the first. Job had more wealth, more children, and more property, cattle and money than he knew what to do with. The bible also says, "In all this Job did not sin."

If you are losing it all, it may not necessarily be because you have sinned. It may be because God is doing something great, better, incredible, and amazing in your life. It may be so that your life can become a testimony throughout the world of what an amazing God can do with one life. Job's life was not over, even though his wife had said, 'curse God and die.' God had a plan for Job's life, and although he had lost everything accept his wife, and three inconsiderate friends, the plan was to give Job back everything he had, and more.

Job's true character came through Job's life during the toughest, darkest times of his life. He still did what he had always done, prayed and talked things over with His God. He did not bash his friends nor did he retaliate against anyone. He did not lash out in anger or cause strife with his wife. He simply went and talked to God for a while about all that was going on in his heart.

There were certain attitudes, and mind sets that Job had in the way he handled his friends, and how he handled losing it all. These are the same actions that we need to take when we are faced with uncertain times in our life. Job talked to God continuously, listened to what God said. He did some intense soul searching during that time. Job also was very real with his friends and with God. He responded to the situation and did not react. He was not over emotional or rude.

He acted in the power of the Holy Spirit. He acted with love and gave grace to his friends.

We need to adopt Job's character in our own life. Job was considered by God a righteous man. Righteousness is based on our believing what God says to be true and us living accordingly to His word.

Job listened intently to God throughout his life. At the end of Job, Job says, "I had heard of you, but now my eyes have seen you." What an amazing thought to ponder. Job, the most righteous man, did not know God as well as he thought. It took some struggles for Job to know God intimately. After Job humbled himself, confessed his sin and prayed for his friends then God gave Job back more.

God gave Job back more than Job could have possibly imagined. If anyone had a, 'right' to be consumed with fear it would have been Job. Yet Job's character manifested itself in the most challenging times of his life. He sought God and talked to God about his troubles. God gave Him more than he had previously.

Everything in our life comes from the Lord, and God gives, and God takes away, blessed be the name of the Lord. May we all get to know God more intimately.

Questions:

1. What friends in your life have given you bad advice?
2. What friends in your life have given you good advice?
3. Have you considered praying for those friends who gave you bad advice?
4. Will you now pray for those friends who have given you bad advice?
5. Have you considered thanking God for your friends that give you good advice?
6. Will you now thank God for those friends that have given you good advice?
7. What have you lost in your life?

Quiet Time:

Will you take time to share with the Lord what it is like for you during your times of stress, struggle and fear.

Talk to God about your fears, and let Him know exactly how you feel about your fears.

Pray for those people that have persecuted you.

Talk to God about your grief, and ask Him to help you let it go.

Day 19

Fear of not having a Plan

Psalms 40:5 Many O Lord my God, are the wonders you have done. The things you planned for us no one can recount to you: were I to speak and tell of them, they would be too many to declare.

The God that created the universe has plans for you. God's plans and decisions are made and designed just for you! You don't need to fret about not having the perfect plan for your life. You don't need to fear that your past failures determine your future. God has a plan and He want to let you in on it!

Have you ever built a house and designed the plans for the house? You are *God's design* and He has a plan for your life.

What is the highest number on the planet? What is the highest number you can count? Whatever that number is, no one can recount to God the things that have been planned for your life!

God has numerous plans for you. When a builder has a set of plans, he does many things to get the house built. When the house is complete, everything is new, beautiful, clean, fresh and delightful to move into.

Do you feel as though you have to have a plan for everything? Are you a control freak? Do you plan out every detail of your life? Do you long for things to go your way and if they don't you don't handle it too well?

You can cease striving and know that He is God. God longs to plan out things for you and longs to make them happen for you. You don't have to try to control things and plans things so much so that you can't enjoy your life if that plan doesn't come to fruition.

God's plans are better than our plans and will come to pass better than we can hope for or expect.

God is re-building your life. The plans that He has for you are too numerous and wonderful for you to even fathom. As you seek Him during these days, ask the builder of your life what is the next phase of the plan.

God knows where you are and He wants to give you a house with a view. He wants your heart to be so clean, new, pure, lovely, beautiful, and fresh that people around you won't even know who this new person is.

Allow the builder to build what He wants out of your life. Follow the plan, and write it down so that in the future you can tell others about all that the Lord did in your life during this time.

The builder of your life is knocking on the door of your heart, and wants to come in, and clean it up, and re-build it.

Have you ever watched a child for a long period of time? They are so filled with wonder, and amazement at every single thing. They are mesmerized at life. They have no thought that life is not amazing. They wake up every day ready to go play outside, and see the world that has been laid out before them. They look at everything with wonder, amazement, and jubilee.

This is the life that God has for you. He has many new and amazing things that He has planned for your life. All you must do is take the Father's hand, and let Him lead.

Hark, a builder is at your door. Fear not. Take His hand, and let Him show you the plans.

Questions:

1. Are you a control freak?
2. Are you a planner?
3. Can you live your life without a plan?
4. Are there any times in your life where you plan hasn't come to pass?
5. How has that effected your day or your life?
6. Does your planning cause discord or strife with others?
7. Does it cause problems with others in your life if your plan doesn't go the way you want it?
8. Have you ever thought about the fact that being such a planner, where it dominates your lives and the lives of others is sin if not submitted to God? *(see next chapter)*
9. Do you submit your plans to God when you make your plans?

Quiet Time:

Submit your plans to God.

Take out a large white plain sheet of paper, some markers, pencils and whatever else you can find to write with. Take time to draw a set of plans of what you would like your life to be like. This is the time to dream, draw, and make plans!

Now after doing that, give it over to God. Tell Him to be in charge of these plans. Ask God to make your dreams happen.

Now after doing that, take out another sheet of paper, and do some drawings of what your life would be like without fear.

For example, if you are afraid of spiders, make a drawing of yourself killing lots of spiders. If you are afraid of flying, make a drawing of you in an airplane.

Give that drawing to God, and ask Him to help you not be afraid of those things anymore, and that you really want to be the person in that picture!

Share the drawings with someone!

Day 20

Fear of others-not being able to Trust

Proverbs 3:5&6 Trust in the Lord with all your heart and lean not on your own understanding in all your ways <u>acknowledge </u>Him, and He will make your paths straight.

I f you've been hurt before, and we all have, it will be hard for you to trust. Trust, once it's broken, is hard to have re-built in your life. If you believe God has hurt you, then it will be a challenge for you to trust Him.

The pieces of your heart have probably been broken by a loved one or the economy during these days of uncertainty in our world. So if your heart has been broken, you may be holding onto pieces your heart, instead of letting it all go to God, and again, especially if you blame God for these struggles you are in.

Blaming God doesn't help. Blame leads to shame and that be-comes a never ending cycle. When you begin to blame God you miss what it is that He has for you in the midst of the trial. God wants to develop your character. If you don't blame God but ask Him what it is He wants you to learn during this difficult time you will be amazed at what He shows you.

The devil, the destroyer, the accuser, is the mean one, not God. God's plans for us are always for our good, and are always for our best interest.

If you are a parent then you understand this. You understand that you want what is best for your child but sometimes your child is disobedient. This probably grieves you when they disobey because you know what you are telling them is for their own good. Yet your child does not listen or trust your judgment and that gets frustrating for you.

God as our parent wants what is best for us. Since His time is not our time and since His ways are not our ways then what He does is in conjunction with eternity and not with the earthly matters or concerns. If you look up at the stars and see the twinkling of them at night, then picture it the other way around. Picture those stars looking down at us and what we must look like to those stars. When God sees us we are but a little tiny dot on the planet. Yet, He cares for us so much so, more than the flowers or the field or the birds of the air that He longs for us to have relationship with Him and trust Him.

Your own understanding of things may not be accurate, especially if you have been hurt and do not trust anyone but yourself. Your own understanding may have a flawed perception and could make your understanding not accurate. The devil could be attacking you with his lies of deception.

God is for you and not against you. You can trust Him. I think during these days many are talking about the economy. The verse does not say, "Trust in the economy with all your heart." It says trust in God with all your heart. We will see during these days who is really born-again and who is not. We will see what we really trust and believe.

The verse does not say, 'and lean on your own understanding.' We are to lean not on our own understanding. We are to ask God to give us new, and right understanding of things. We are to get His understanding and perspective of things.

The verse says in all your ways. Imagine if you had a father that you could call up for advice any time you needed it, and he would give you exactly the right answer, at the right time, for the right issue you were facing. You have that in God. You Heavenly Father wants you to acknowledge Him moment by moment, especially in your decision making process. Your ways will become straight paths, as you take His hand, and He leads.

I think God knows and is aware of the economy. He is not surprised by anything happening in our world today. He knows, and is fully aware. We can trust Him through it all.

In Hebrew the word trust means:

Batach:

Refuge, confident, sure, bold, hope

In Greek the word trust means:

Biotikos:

Relating to the present existence-pertaining to things that are of this life

So, we can create our own definition based on the original meaning of the word.

In this present life we can take refuge in our Lord Jesus Christ! You can be confident and sure of the fact that God is on your side. You can be bold in your prayers to Him. You can have hope that God is not asleep. He is in this present life and longs to give you the best of life.

Questions:

1. Who do you trust?
2. Who don't you trust?
3. Who has hurt you?
4. How have they hurt you?

5. How has your trust been broken?
6. Do you acknowledge Him in all things from where you will go to college to who you will marry to what car you will buy to what job you will take?
7. Do you submit your daily plans to Him?
8. Do you submit your finances to Him-what you spend or don't spend?

Quiet Time:

Take one step this week to have your trust be re-built. For example: If you don't trust your spouse, ask the Lord to remove all conflict between you and your spouse. If you don't trust your boss, put an empty chair in front of you and pretend your boss was sitting there. Tell your boss all the things you want to really say to them (this is the time to yell, shout, and be straight with your boss.) When you are finished, ask God to remove all doubt and fear concerning your boss.

If your trust issue is severe, call a person you do trust, like a Pastor, and make a counseling appointment

I heard someone say once, "Trust can not be built in conflict." If there is conflict with your boss, your spouse, your friend, or whomever, do what ever it is you can do to get that conflict removed. This is not an overnight process, this is a lengthy process. You may need to confront a person, or you may just need to pray.

Find a brick, or a rock, and picture that conflict with that person while you are holding the rock or brick. Now, go somewhere where you can scream, whether it is the beach, a mountain top, or in your back yard. Hold up that brick or rock while you are screaming about the conflict, and throw the brick or rock down and out of your life, permanently.

As conflict is removed in your life, so does fear. Fear and conflict co-exist together, and having lack of trust in your life also causes one to have fear. Trust issues need to be dealt with.

Begin every single morning submitting and acknowledging the Lord and giving to Him every move you make for that day. Watch Him begin to work mightily in your life and having all the plans succeed.

Day 21

Fear of Trouble

Ecclesiastes 11:10 So then, banish anxiety from your heart and cast off the troubles of your body, for youth and vigor are meaningless.

Anxiety is a heart issue, not a circumstance issue. Anxiety comes from our thoughts, which filter down into our heart.

The writer here was King Solomon himself. He was filled with wisdom from God Himself. Solomon was saying that it does not do any good to be anxious and that we can cast off the troubles from our body and our heart.

Anxiety is rooted in fear. Fear comes from not trusting in God. Fear may very well also come from trust in our self, and not in God Himself. For if we are trusting in ourselves, and our circumstances from all around us fail, we blame ourselves. Then we have fear, and don't want to make future decisions based on that fear.

God gave me a vision once while I was afraid. I was laying on the couch looking at the fireplace. The vision was that the fire that was burning was burning me up from the inside of my fearful soul. There were roots of fear deep in my soul, and that fire was burning up the roots. Then, God in His healing power came in and replenished my fearful soul, and He became my all consuming fire and all anxiety banished from my heart.

My fear had come out of me depending on my husband, the economy, and myself for meeting my needs. My deep rooted fear was because I was trying to depend on my husband's abilities and my own to pay our bills. I did not have a deep fear of God. My fear of losing it all came from depending upon myself, not God.

If we are depending upon God and we lose it all, we can trust it will all be ok. If we lose it all, and we are depending on our own strength to get it back again, we need to repent, banish that anxiety from our heart, get rid of it, and have *God consume us*, not our fear.

Banish is an action word and so is cast off. It is a choice whether we are anxious or not. We can make a choice, with the all-consuming fire, who burns up the root of our fear, to have peace instead of anxiety.

Have your decisions been based on God and what He wants you to do? If your decisions have been based on God then there is no reason to fear. You can have peace knowing that He is your direction. If your decisions have been made on your own, without the direction from God, it's time to repent, ask God to consume you with His fire, and burn up the deep root of fear in your life. Fear is doing nothing but making you, and all those you love, miserable.

Questions:

1. Have you had anxiety attacks lately?
2. What is making you anxious?
3. Do you think about what you think about?
4. Did you know that you can control your thoughts?
5. When you are anxious do you stop to think about what you are thinking about and change your thought pattern?

Quiet Time:

The next time you feel anxiety come upon you, think immediately what your mind is thinking about, and write it down. Change the negative thought to a positive one. For example: If your thought is, "I am so afraid I can not do this transaction at work right." Change that to "I can do this right, and even if I make a mistake, the Lord can help me learn, correct the mistake and move on."

You have control of your thought life. get a notebook specifically for what you think about. When you have time this week, take some time to jot down what it is you have been thinking about, and change them into positive statements. For example: If you think, "Why is that person acting so rude?" Change that thought in your notebook to, "I give that person the benefit of the doubt, they must be having a bad day, and I won't let their day, ruin mine."

The above exercises take discipline to do. You may need to take your lunch hour to do them once or twice this week, just to get an idea of what you think about.

Day 22

Fear of not having the Perfect Wedding

Song of Solomon 2:4 He's brought me to His Banquet Table, His Banner over me (and you) is love

What the world needs now, is love, sweet love was the song that I had playing while my husband and I cut our wedding cake. There is a story behind that wedding cake.

My friend had offered to make our wedding cake for a wedding gift. She lived in South Carolina, a few hours from our place, and would drive up the day before, make it and get it to the reception in time. Allison's sister, (the girl who volunteered to make our wedding cake), Angie was my best friend since seventh grade. We were so delighted when she offered to do this for us.

Thursday night I got a call and was not able to answer the phone due to family just arriving. I listened to my voice mail on Friday morning at about 7:00 am and the message sounded urgent. It was from my friend Angie from Junior High, "Please call me as soon as you can."

I called at 7:15 am. I knew she would be up because she had children. She answered, and began saying that her sister Allison would not be able to come and make our cake because her car had broken down. I listened to the long story while my bride's maid, Kate, sat on the other sofa sipping her coffee and praying.

The evening before my fiancé and I had gotten in an argument, and he had left rather irritated, so I sure did not expect to see him bright and early Friday morning. While on the phone, I heard someone at the door. To my and Kate's surprise, it was David, my fiancé, coming over to have coffee with us! I put my friend on hold and said, "Um, honey, I'm talking to Angie. We don't have a wedding cake. Our friend's car broke down and she can't make it." He said, "Get Alison on the phone."

I kept speaking to Angie and hung up. The further Kate, David and I talked, the further I knew that David had to speak to Allison. We called back and David said to Allison, "I will do whatever it takes to get you up here. I will put a rental car on my charge card and pay for your gas so you can come here. Whatever it takes; my fiancé wants you to make her cake." The further they talked the further I saw his face saddened.

Now mind you, he hadn't even had his coffee yet and he was already at work on his fiancé's behalf! We live in the Outer Banks of North Carolina, which is a big bride area. You can not get a cake for cheaper than about $400.00 a cake. Plus, it was Memorial Day weekend a very hectic bridal weekend in the Outer Banks!

We had no clue what to expect next.

David got the phone book out while Kate and I sipped our coffee and prayed. He called the Harris Teeter grocery store! He was pacing back and forth on the deck and occasionally he would open the door and say, "Ok honey, what do you want on the cake? Get whatever you want."

Harris Teeter made an exception that day. They don't make wedding cakes. My fiancé, now husband, went to bat for me, (and him), and hustled to get us a wonderful wedding cake.

On Saturday morning my groom went to pick up our beautiful wedding cake Harris Teeter! To this day thinking about it makes me cry. I was getting dressed at the reception place when he showed up carrying the most beautiful cake in the world up those stairs! All who saw the groom carrying the cake said it was priceless. (NO- he didn't see me!)

Months before we had picked out our cake cutting song, how appropriate it would be. "What the world needs now, is love sweet love, it's the only thing that there's just too little of!"

It was not in the original plan to spend three hours on Friday morning dealing with wedding cake drama. The day before the wedding had been planned out minute by minute. Yet the plans got change and we all had to be content with the new plan. Sometimes in life plans get altered and they are not at all what we expect yet the One who created us has our best interest at heart and He will help us get through changing times. When things don't go our way we just need to pray. We all need to learn to be ok with interruptions and time tables that are not going according to our plan.

No one at the reception except a few friends knew of the ordeal. The best part is that when my groom went to pick up the cake, it had been paid for by some other friends that knew of what had happened!

David, Kate and I-and all of us-enjoyed our reception with the most beautiful cake in the world, compliments of the groom and some wonderful friends! Oh, and Jesus Himself was with us all along.

Jesus Christ has a wedding banquet prepared for you and will give you more than your heart's desire. He continuously knocks on the door of your heart and says, "Honey, what do you want?" He wants to give you a beautiful, delicious wedding feast with you and all your friends! His banner over you is love! He wants to give you a great feast, with all your friends and loved ones included!

Don't fear over the cake you don't have, become delighted in the cake that King Jesus, your husband, your groom wants to give you! It will be delicious, and delightful! When we get to heaven, the only thing that will be in heaven is each other. WE won't have our things with us. WE can enjoy them while we are here, but all that the Kingdom is ever about is people, and how we treated them, and what we did for them.

Loving others, even in the midst of challenging times, is the best gift you can ever give to someone. Love casts out all fear!

He has your wedding planned, prepared, and has your wedding cake all picked out! Just for you!

Questions:

1. What would your ideal wedding cake be like, taste like, look like, if money was not a concern?
2. Where would your ideal wedding be, if money was not a concern?
3. What would your wedding reception table look like if money was not a concern?
4. How can you show someone this week that you love them?
5. How can you show yourself this week that you love you?

Quiet Time:

Talk to God about your wedding day and how you would like it to be. If you are married discuss with Him how you were happy with your wedding or disappointed with your wedding. If there is anyone you need to forgive for how they hurt you doing your wedding planning or on your day forgive them and share that with God.

Prepare a nice meal for yourself, and your spouse if you are married. Get some fresh flowers, light the candles, set the table with fine china. Pretend that this is God setting you up for a beautiful, wonderful, wedding feast in eternity. You can get dressed up also. You don't have to do this in your home, you can get a picnic together and take it to a beautiful place with your spouse or a friend. This is a feast for you, so get some of your favorite foods, and enjoy them, and thank God for them. Share them with someone you love.

God is saying to you, "Honey what do you want?" Well, what do you want? To be free from fear? Tell God what you want in your life! God is preparing you for the ultimate wedding, the one with Him in eternity!

Day 23

Fear of not having the best from God

Isaiah 1:19 "If you are willing and obedient, you will eat the best from the land."

G ot fruit?
God wants to give you the best of the land in your life, whatever that land may be. However, you must be willing, and you must be obedient.

Americans love junk food. We love chocolate, ice cream, and McDonald's cheeseburgers. We love hot dogs, milk-shakes, apple pie, fried dough, and cinnamon rolls. We love orange danishes, waffles, pancakes, peanut butter, and cookies. The list goes on. We forget about clementines, pineapple, apples, bananas, kiwi, strawberries, oranges, grapes, grapefruit, and more.

I think you have heard the expression, "garbage in, garbage out." If you fill up with junk food before dinner, you won't eat your vegetables. If we pig out on bon-bons, we will miss out on the delicious kiwi that God has for us. Junk food crowds out what it is that God wants to do in our lives. Junk food could be too much television, those wrong negative friends we all have, wrong choices, decisions, and most of all wrong thinking that paralyzes us with fear.

God never intended junk food to crowd out his best for our lives. Funny thing is, we make the choice to eat junk before dinner. Dinner is the powerful stuff. Dinner is the deep things of God that He wants to give us. Dinner is meat and potatoes! Dinner is the substance of life!

The word eat means in Greek

Anaphaino: *Should appear, Discover*

Hebrew it means

Akal-Burn up, consume, devour, dine, freely, wise, meat

The word land in Greek means:

Asitia: *Fasting, abstinence*

In Hebrew it means:

Erets: *The earth, country, field, nations, ground, wilderness, world*

We can come up with a few of our own sentences here. Let us ponder the word, and come up with something to chew on!

If you abstain from junk food, you will eat the meat of this great world of ours, and dine with Kings in the nations of the world!

Or, how about this:

If you fast from wrong thinking, negative friends, television, and ice cream, you will consume the earth, the nations, and the world. You will be able to make better decisions in your life that will benefit you and your relationship with God, if you fast from negativity!

Or, well you get the idea. Willing, obedient. IF YOU. You have to make the choices in your life to get what God has for you. God is not Santa Claus. He gives us free will to choose but we can choose whichever way we want to go. Which aisle at the grocery store we want to go down; the ice cream aisle or the produce aisle?

Do you want to produce the best of the land in your life that God has to offer? Eat more kiwi.

I heard a personal trainer say to me once, "If you are craving sugar, it means you are craving fruit."

Do not fear, for God has the best of the land for you and your life! *Got fruit?*

Questions*:*

1. What is your favorite junk food?
2. What is your favorite fruit?
3. Where in the world would you love to go, if money was not a concern?
4. What are you willing to do for God?
5. If you could have dinner with any King in the world, past or present, who would it be and why would you want to dine with them?
6. What questions would you ask that King?
7. What food would you want on the table with the King?

Quiet Time:

Make a basket of fruit for yourself. Every day this week eat a piece of fruit. As the fruit is going down inside of you, tell God that you want to bear fruit in your life, and that you want to abstain from the junk of this world.

Day 24

Fear of God not knowing You Intimately

Jeremiah 1:5 Before you were in your mother's womb, I knew you.

Almighty, all loving, all powerful, amazing, wonderful, counselor, creator knows you. He knows all about you. He knows who your mother is!

He planted you right inside her womb, and put you there for a purpose, a plan, a life.

He did not put you there for death, destruction, negativity, and to live it with fear.

The word before in the Hebrew Language means:

Terem: *not yet*

The word knew in the Hebrew Language means:

Yada: *A great variety of senses. Instruction. Designation. Acknowledge. Advise. Answer. Appoint. Assuredly. Be aware. Certainly. Certainty. Comprehend. Consider. Declare. Be familiar. Discern. Diligent. Be familiar. Friend. Famous. Feel. Can have. Instruct. Kinsman. To make. To know. To lie by man. Respect. To understand.*

Now those words are powerful. This is not just a, oh I know the person I work with, or I know my mail man, or I know my neighbor but never hang out with them. This is a powerful knowing. He is familiar with you. He has felt you and He respects you. God understand you and wants to advise you. He is aware of you, HE comprehends you, and He wants you to be famous for His name sake.

To emphasize the point we can make up some great sentences.

When you were not yet in existence on this earth God Almighty wanted to be your friend. When you were not yet on this earth God felt you and had feelings for you. When you were not yet on this earth He wanted to declare to the world He was creating such a beautiful person. When you were not yet a breathing human being God respected you and considered you. The best part is that *God actually respects* you.

This is someone who knows you more than your best friend.

When no one else thought about you, God did. If you have been told you were a mistake it is a lie from the pit of hell itself.

God knows you intimately and personally. He knows where you live. God knows everything about you. He knows you better than anyone on the earth.

God wants you to know Him in the same way. Yes, God is Spirit and you can not see Him. Yet you can now Him so personally, so intimately, so closely that it will change your life forever. He is a good loving God.

The family I was born into was not perfect. My dad went to prison when I was a toddler, and I did not know it until I was in my twenties. I did not go to meet him until I was in my thirties. My mom worked three jobs at times to put meat on our table, (spam at its best) and we got no child support.

God knew all of this, and God wants to use me to tell the world about His love, grace, forgiveness, mercy, and more. God knew who my mother would be, and God knows your mother.

You were planted in your family for a reason. They may drive you nuts. You may not like them at times. You may not even want to be around them at Christmas, however, God wants to use what the enemy came to stole, and redeem it for His purpose and plan.

Maybe your mother was an alcoholic; God may want to use you to minister to children of alcoholics. Maybe your mother was verbally abusive, maybe God wants to use you to speak healing into people's lives, and use your voice for healing. Maybe you didn't get many hugs when you were growing up, God may want to use you to be the best hugger in the world.

Don't let satan rob you of your future. Allow God to use whatever it is in your life that is broken. He wants to mend it, and use you mightily to help others.

He knows where you are right now. Why don't you pray and cry out to Him to allow Him to use you? Allow Him to do whatever it is in your life that is needed to bring about His purpose for your life. His purpose is better than whatever it is you can create for yourself. Ask Him to plant dreams inside of you that are *His* dreams for you. He is your loving Father and He wants to use you. Let Him.

Do not fear, God isn't finished with you yet!

Questions:

1. Do you like your family?
2. Who in your family annoys you?
3. What have they done to hurt you?
4. Have you hurt anyone in your family?
5. Who in your family do you need to forgive?

<u>Quiet Time:</u>

Write a letter of apology to anyone in your family that you need to forgive. This letter is not a bashing letter, however it can say in it whatever it is you need to get off your chest. Do not give it to them, or mail it to them unless you feel led. This is a letter that you write and give that letter to God.

Day 25

Fear of Remaining in the Pit

Lamentations 4: 55-57 I called your name, O Lord, from the depths of the pit. You heard my plea: "Do not close your ears to my cry for relief." You came near when I called you, and you said, "Do not fear."

Dark, dreary, barren, stark, gray, and lonely is the land of Mongolia. I was there right after 9/11. As I stood on the mountain and looked over the land, I cried out to the Lord on behalf of the Mongolian people, 'Where does their help come from, but from you O Lord.' Then, I got to really looking at that land and the closer I looked, I saw fear. The people of Mongolia were filled with fear and they had every reason to be filled with that fear. The land has no vegetation, no clean water, and it gets very cold in winter. I remember sleeping in a gair, which looks like a big round tent with a wood stove with lots of people when I was there. It was winter and it was cold. The 'bathroom' was a pit in the back.

That pit was stinky and dark. It smelled like fear all around that Mongolian land. That pit in the back changed my life forever. It was a picture of fear. I remember looking down into that pit and it was a long way down and it was dark. You couldn't see far down that pit and all you saw was darkness. I couldn't wait to get away from that pit. Many nights I had to wander out to that pit to use it. I dreaded going out to that pit to use it in the middle of the night. It was a fearful situation.

I imagine that at times our soul feels like it is as lonely as that Mongolian pit in the back. Our souls at times are so lonely, dark and dreary. I can only imagine myself getting stuck down in that pit for days upon end without hopes for escaping it. That would definitely be a dreadful situation. That is how many people today are living their lives. They are in a stinky pit of despair and it looks like a dreadful Mongolian pit all alone in the back.

I remember visiting the cave people while we were there. These people were the outcasts of the land. We traveled for miles before we arrived at our destination. We climbed down into the cave and there were people in there! This was also a picture of a pit to me.

The beds were of rock and the lady of the house offered us broth in a rock. To her, she was giving us her best. A Mongolian preacher pulled out his guitar and we began singing, "Lord I life your name on high, Lord I love to sing your praises, I'm so glad you're in my life, I'm so glad you came to save us." They were singing in Mongolian, we were singing in English, my eyes filled up with tears.

Those Mongolian people are living in a pit and are calling out to God!

They are so glad God is in their life because that is all they truly have. They sleep on a bed of rock in a dark cave, where the only light they get is the light from the hole above the cave. They have made for themselves shelter from the storm, and they worship God there. I know God hears them!

<u>The word Heard in the Hebrew Language means:</u>

Shama: To hear intelligently. Attention. Obedience. Attentively. Call together. Carefully. Certainty. Consent. Consider. Be content. Declare. Diligently. Discern. Give ear. Hear. Indeed. Listen. Make a noise. Perceive. Proclaim. Publish. Regard. Report. Shew forth. Surely. Tell. Understand. Whosoever heareth. Witness an intelligent God gives you undivided attention when you call on Him. He attentively hears, considers and diligently discerns the problem. He is careful with you, and perceives correctly what you are saying to Him.

When a book is published it is a lengthy process. It is not just something that happens over night. It takes sometimes six months to see hard work come into print. God puts your cries, your prayers, your calls unto Him in print. He sees the full picture. He is very detailed and accurate about you.

He puts into literal words what you are saying in prayer to Him. He edits what is not meant to be there, and lovingly reads the words upon your heart to His heart. Your prayers to Him are a perfect manuscript that He has published onto His very heart. You do not need to fear, God does hear.

The land of fear that is in your heart is dreary, dark, cold, damp, lonely, barren, and stark yet if you look up from your dark and lonely state, you can see the light filtering in. There is a little bit of light, and if you just look up, you will see the light shining. The light is the *Son*, trying to warm your cold heart of fear.

He desires to penetrate that heart of yours and have you release your fear unto Him. I know during the days when I was afraid of losing it all, I went back in time to a Mongolian cave and I looked up and saw the light. I began singing praises again to the King, 'Lord I lift your name on high, I'm so glad you're in my life, I'm so glad you came to save us.'

His word tells us in Lamentations that He hears us when we call, and He hears us from the pit of despair! He gently shines His light into the pit of our cave of fear and says, "Do not fear, for I am with you, and I hear your cry for help."

Questions:

1. What is barren in your life?

2. What is cold in your life?
3. What is dark in your life?
4. Do you believe God hears you when you call, even when you sin?

Quiet Time:

If your heart is cold do one thing this week to help you get some warmth in that heart. For example: If you have a hard time dealing with people, say hello to at least one stranger this week and smile at them sincerely. If you are mad at your spouse, do something this week that will shed some light into that situation. Get creative. It could be something as simple as calling your spouse on your break and telling them that you are sorry.

If you are in a secret sin, bring some light into that sin. Talk to the Lord about your secret sin, and if at all possible, call a prayer line on a 1-800 number and confess that secret sin and have someone pray with you for healing.

Take some time when you can to listen to praise and worship music, and sing to the Lord, praises, even if you don't 'feel like it.' This will bring peace into your heart, and light into your life. If you do not have a Christian music cd, you can contact a friend, or someone at a church and ask them to borrow some Christian worship music, and someone will be glad to lend some to you. If you can not get anyone, contact me, and I will get some to you!

Day 26

Fear of others not Listening to You

Ezekiel 2:6 And you, son of man, do not be afraid of them or their words. Do not be afraid, though briers and thorns are all around you and you l live among scorpions. Do not be afraid of what they say or terrified by them, though they are a rebellious house.

Remember Sally, look both ways before crossing the street. Remember Caleb, don't talk to strangers. Remember Sue to be home by 11:00 pm.

A parent repeats themselves several times to get points across to their children-important ones, usually ones that will help them, protect them, encourage them, and bene-fit them. This is what God was saying to Ezekiel. God was mak-ing a point to Ezekiel to not be afraid. I have heard it said that when God wants to make a point, He repeats himself three times; such is the case with Ezekiel.

God had said it several times to Ezekiel and He was re-iterating the point. Do not be afraid, again, I tell you! Ezekiel had a strong call on his life.

Ezekiel was a prophet. His call on his life was to go to the Israe-lites and tell them where they had sinned, and to repent, or else. That is not a very popular calling. Would you go tell someone they needed to repent or else?

This may seem like a small task. However if you read the book of Ezekiel you will find that God says over and over that the Israelites were stubborn, obstinate, and didn't listen. God also tells Ezekiel several times that the Israelites would not even listen to him, and they were going to do mean things to him in the process.

God even warned him several times that the Israelites would not listen to him because they would not listen to God. He gave Ezekiel the call and then He even told Ezekiel that the people wouldn't listen to Ezekiel when he tells them what God had told them! So the Israelites would not listen to Ezekiel or God!

Would that be your dream calling from God? Going to tell people to repent that you know very well are not going to do what you say doesn't sound appealing. Yet, this is exactly what God tells Ezekiel to do with his life.

Now mind you, the Israelites had no clue this was happening. They were in their own little, stubborn, rebellious world, doing their own thing when Ezekiel came to them. They would not listen.

Do you have a call on your life? Has God told you to do something that seems impossible or fearful to you? You may be called to go overseas to do missions. You may be called to the nursing home down the road. You may be called to a prison in tin-buck-two, or you may be called to minister to your husband. Whatever the call is on your life, don't be afraid. If someone doesn't listen, and you know that God has called you to it, don't be afraid. Do the call anyway. God will reward you and bless you. You do not need to be doing things for men's approval but for God's.

During the time that I was afraid of losing it all my husband and I were separated for a few days. Then, my husband came back! My husband was only gone for three days, it was as though we both had a resurrection while he was away.

God had asked me if I was willing and obedient to do whatever it took to make the marriage work and to release my fear of losing it all to God. I have to make an effort every single day of my life to study the word of God on fear, to release that fear to the altar, and do the call of God that is on my life. Currently, that call is to minister to my husband and a hurting world that is fearful.

God is our provider. God will take care of us. No matter what happens, we still have work for the Kingdom of God to do and accomplish. That is something no one can take away from us. No bill collector or no mortgage company can take the Kingdom of God away from you!

Are you willing and obedient to release your fear and do whatever it takes to make your life with God and others work for the glory of God? May we all be like Ezekiel and do whatever it takes; all for the glory of God!

Questions:

1. Has God asked you to do something that you think is impossible?
2. What is God asking of you that seems impossible?
3. What are you facing right now?
4. Do you feel like being obedient to the Lord, moment by moment, daily, in your life?
5. What do you need to do right now, so that you can be more obedient to God?

Quiet Time:

What step do you need to take in your life towards the impossible? For example: If God is asking you to go on a missions trip, how are you going to get the money? Maybe you need to fund raise, or maybe you need to ask someone, or maybe you need to write letters out to people.

Take one step this week towards that. If you think your marriage has no hope left, you need to take one more step to try to repair it. You need to listen to a good marriage seminar, call a prayer line, or sow a seed into a marriage ministry. Do something that is a challenge for, towards your impossible situation!

Day 27

Fear of Lions

Daniel 6: 26 & 27 "For he is the living God, and he endures forever; his kingdom will not be destroyed, his dominion will never end. He rescues and he saves, he performs signs and wonders in the heavens and on the earth. He has rescued Daniel from the power of the lions."

L ions and tigers and bears, oh my! The lions needed courage in the lion's den with Daniel!

<u>The word power in the Hebrew means:</u>

Yad: *An open hand. Both proximate and remot. Axle tree. Armhole. Charge. Creditor. Custody. Debt. Dominion. Handed. Means. Mine. Ministry. Order. Ordinance. Pain. Sumptuously. Service. Side. Sore. State. Stay. Draw with strength. Swear. Terror.*

The power of the lions was fierce. God is called in scripture the Lion of Judah!

It may feel like if you have collectors and creditors calling you trying to collect on past due debt. It seems like those creditors are lions are after you!

Creditors, collectors and bills oh my! God understands and God knows full well that those creditors contacting you at all hours of the night or bright and early in the morning is the same as those Lions that were in that den trying to kill Daniel! God rescued Him from that power, and God will rescue you. It is your re-sponsibility right now to begin praying three times a day, as Daniel did to be delivered and rescued from the power of the collectors.

I am not saying that your debt will be wiped out, although that can happen. I am saying however that God will deliver you from the terror that you feel every single time that phone rings and it is a bill collector.

There were no tigers and bears in that den of lions. It was lions, lions, and more lions and enough lions to kill Daniel in a New York minute.

The enemy, who is Satan, wants your life destroyed, not God. Satan prowls around the earth, seeking for someone to devour. In Daniel's case, he had been falsely accused, and then broke the decree which said a person could not pray to God, yet Daniel prayed three times a day to God. In the scripture we read that, The scriptures that when Daniel heard of the decree passed, to not worship His God, Daniel went to his upstairs room and, prayed three times a day, just as he had done before. Daniel seemed to not be afraid.

The King came to Daniel threw him in the Lion's Den and locked the door. He then put a large stone over the door. The King says to Daniel through that stone, "May your God rescue you." I can hear the King say it with sarcasm.

Why did Daniel get put into a den of Lions? Because he was a man who was a prayer warrior.

Can you see it now? Someone throws you into a den of lions, and as they lock the door they shout out loud, "Hope your God rescues you!"

It would seem at that moment in time that Daniel had lost it all. To those on the outside world the King and others thought, "Daniel won't survive this. He is as good as dead. His life is over. Daniel, the praying man, is now dead. The lions of life are bigger than Daniel's God."

The people were wrong.

God shuts the mouths of the lions by sending an angel to Daniel. Daniel was in the den all night long with those Lions, just hanging out, with the lions mouths closed!

The next day the King came to see if Daniel's God had rescued him, and He had! The King issued a new decree that all people must worship Daniel's God, Amen! Daniel was gone. A new decree was signed, sealed, delivered!

The Lion of Judah Himself had rescued Daniel from the den of lions. The Lion of Judah Himself, shut the mouths up of the lions in the den. I bet those lions were shaking in their paws, and needed some courage. I bet that the Lion of Judah commanded them harshly to shut up their mouths and leave His son Daniel, alone!

Perhaps you have been betrayed, like Daniel, by others who have lied about you behind your back; told your boss that you did something at work that you did not do and now you are being put on probation. Perhaps your husband has lied to you about a very major issue, or your sibling has lied to your parents about something you did not say and you are being disciplined. Perhaps at a church function someone lied about you all in the matter of a prayer chain phone call, and exaggerated your prayer to others and now, you are being looked at accusingly by all at church. Perhaps, someone went to your Pastor, lied about you, and you are being ex-communicated from the church without cause.

Perhaps you feel like your life is over, and people have shut you out, locked the door, put a stone over your heart and life and are screaming at you, "Yeah, let's see if your God can rescue you now." Maybe you are even questioning your God.

Lions are all around us. They could be our spouse, our friend, our boss, our co-worker, a person at the post office yelling at you in line, or your very own mother, father, sister, brother, or child. Lions attack us when we least expect them, and get us when we are vulnerable. Lions are big, hairy, and burly. They have a reputation for roaring loudly and whether you want them to roar or be quiet, they still roar.

Picture your boss roaring at you, an employee roaring at you, your wife, your husband, or a stranger in the midst of road rage! These are all the lions of our lives and they come at times when we least expect them.

Daniel had no idea that he would be thrown into the lion's den, neither did you. You did not expect your business to fail, your finances to collapse, disappear, or your spouse to have an affair. These are all lions in our lives that leave us vulnerable, and afraid.

The lions of our lives can destroy us or develop us. They can make us into a Daniel of our day or turn us into a defeated downcast depressed damsel in distress waiting for a rescuer to come. The Lion of Judah wants to be the One who rescues you.

Don't be afraid, just pray! Pray continuously and you will be delivered. It took the King all night before he came back to check on Daniel to see if Daniel's God had delivered him. It must have seemed like an eternity to Daniel, being in that Lion's den all night long, not knowing if anyone would come back and check on him. Yet he prayed. While the mouths of the lions were shut, Daniel prayed in that lions den, without food or water, all night long. Then the King came, opened up that cellar door, let Daniel out, and issued a new decree!

Your fear is your fear, your pain is your pain. No one can take that away from you except Christ alone. Allow Him to begin removing the fear in your life and once removed, you will be victorious in the circumstance and situation you are facing.

A new decree is coming into your life. If you just continuously humble yourself in your darkest midnight hour then the Lion of Judah, the rescuer, will deliver you from the power of the Lions. God is more powerful than the Lion of your life. Pray to Him, and you will be delivered!

Questions:

1. Who are the lions of your life?
2. What situation or circumstance in your life do you consider a lion?
3. What keeps growling at you, or who keeps growling at you?
4. What is overwhelming you?

<u>Quiet Time:</u>

Pray three times this week for the lions of your life to be shut up.

Ask the Lion of Judah to deliver you from the lions mouths

If you need courage today for a certain situation, or circumstance, picture lions eating up the negative situation and circumstance in your life, and then picture the Lion of Judah, a beautiful Lion, like the one in the Lion King, and picture Him looking at you, smiling at you, loving you. Get the courage you need from the Lion of Judah who is right there with you. If you must, go get the Lion King movie, and watch it again, and picture the Lion King in that movie as the Lion of Judah rescuing and delivering you from the mouth of the lions

If you can, go find a little tiny lion, and put it by your bed, or some place where you can see it continuously, to remind you that the Lion of Judah is shutting the mouths of the lions of fear, etc., in your life.

Day 28

Fear of no Hope

Hosea 2: 14 & 15 "Therefore I am now going to allure her; I will lead her into the desert and speak tenderly to her. There I will give her back her vineyards, and will make the Valley of Achor a door of hope. There she will sing as in the days of her youth, as in the day she came up out of Egypt."

Whether we admit it or not, we all want to be allured. There are plenty of movies and songs about romance, hearts, and flowers. We desire to be allured, taken away, romanced by the one we love.

The word allured in Webster's means:

To attract with something desirable, entice. To be highly, often subtly attractive. The power to attract.

The word Achor in the Hebrew means: *Troubled!*

When God had me look that up in my own devotional time it said that Achor means troubled. I was floored! This is so profound.

God wants to turn the Valley of Trouble (Trouble as known as Achor) in your life into hope!

Isn't that wonderful, glorious, enticing news! You may feel as though you are in a Valley of trouble, however God is going to turn it into an open door, a wide open door of hope for you! This is His promise to you in His word!

God wants to entice you, be attractive to you, and use His power to allure you by turning your trouble into hope.

Hosea had been commanded by God to marry a prostitute. The story is a beautiful story of redemption, forgiveness, and love. That was the point of God's command to Hosea, to show the Israelites how much they were loved by God.

Gomer was Hosea's wayward wife. She left him several times for cheating on the other side of town and Hosea took her back every single time. At times, he even goes looking for her to bring her home! In the end, she and Hosea were restored, grace and forgiveness had been extended, and love renewed.

God loves Israel and us the same way. This story is a picture of how we have committed adultery against God. We have all sinned against Him and we have all had other loves in our lives besides God. We have all allowed other things to come in the way of our relationship with God. This is all like cheating on God in a way for if other things take God's place in our lives those things are idols. We have all squandered time, money and done things that are contrary to the word of God. Yet God takes us back every single time.

No matter our sins, or how many times we sin, God loves us, and wants what is best for us. He desires for us to be healed, loved, forgiven, and have the best of the vineyards that He has for us.

There is a cry in the human heart to be allured. I have heard many scholars debate this issue and state that marriage is not all hearts and flowers. Marriage is definitely challenging. Yet through the scriptures we read about God's alluring love towards us, and that, my friend, is where we can get the hearts and flowers of our lives and hearts, from God, and God alone. Only God can turn a troubled heart to His heart. If you are losing everything you own, or if you are losing a relationship you long for, if you are losing your job, if you are losing anything of value to you, if you are losing your sanity, peace, joy, and seem to be headed for the desert, praise the Lord! He is alluring you to the desert, and it is there, if you allow Him to, He will speak tenderly to you! You can lie on your back at night, on the sand, and look up at the twinkling stars, and be quiet, still and listen to God speak to you, tenderly, romantically, and lovingly! If you are in the process of losing things, people, or your mind, God wants to remove the distractions of your life so that what is His will in your life can come to fruition! He wants the vineyards of apples, grapes, and new wine to come into your life and that can not happen with all the old stuff of your life getting in the way.

He is bringing you to the desert, for a wonderful, alluring reason. He is going to forgive you there, woo you there, love on you there, and minister to you there. I am not suggesting that one has to go to the dessert to be allured by God. I am saying that if you are heading to a desert place, fear not. Watch God do something wonderful for you while you are in the desert place of your life!

Our fear of loss is not only monetary. Our fear of loss can consist of many different situations, circumstances, and scenarios of our life. Loss is loss, whether it is monetary or not. Whatever it is you are losing, do not let someone else tell you it is not a big deal. It is a big deal to you whatever it is you are losing, and God understands that. Many people may have told Hosea that who cares if his wayward wife never comes back. What's the big deal if he lost her? Well, it was a big deal, because God had commanded him to marry her, and he knew that whether anyone else believed him! He was sure of the will of God in his life, and having a wayward wife was no easy task. However, he obeyed God, and God blessed them in the end.

Whatever you are losing right now, and if you are headed to the desert, fear not, don't be afraid. God loves you and is alluring you to the desert place, the empty place, the barren space, the dryness of your soul, heart, mind and He is going to do miraculous things in you and through you during this time.

Hosea was faithful to his wayward wife, his troubled wife, even when she was not. God is faithful to you, no matter if you have been faithful or not. God is faithful to you and knows all your troubles and will turn them into a door of hope!

Questions:

1. What troubles you?
2. Have you ever thought God was not there for you?
3. Have you ever lost faith in God?
4. Have you ever considered that God has never left you, nor forsaken you, especially in times of trouble?

Quiet Time:

Take one night this week to look up at the stars for a long time. Perhaps you will even see a shooting star. Ponder, consider, and reflect on all those stars. Consider the fact that you are God's super star, and He is with you in your trouble. Talk to the Lord while you are looking at the stars. If possible, take a telescope out there. If not, take your journal, a head lamp on your head, and a pen and write out what God tells you while you are looking at the stars.

Consider, ponder, and reflect on this week how God can possibly turn your trouble into hope, how can God turn this around for you?

If possible, watch the movie Pretty Woman this month with the girls. Watch it from a Christian perspective.

As you watch, consider that the Lord is Richard Gear, and you are Julia Roberts. Watch how he acts towards her, during her state she is in as a prostitute, and watch Richard take her, allure her, and fall in love with her. This is how God loves you and what He wants to do in your life.

Day 29

Fear of the Economy

Joel 2: 12-14 & 21. "Even now," declares the Lord, return to me with all your heart, with fasting and weeping and mourning." Rend your heart and not your garments. Return to the Lord your God, for he is gracious and compassionate, slow to anger and abounding in love. Who knows, he may turn and have pity and leave behind a blessing –grain offerings, and drink offerings for the Lord your God. Be not afraid, O land; be glad and rejoice. Surely the Lord has done great things.

*E*ven now, in the midst of our economic turmoil, trouble, and scaring tactics that we watch on TV, we can trust our God. We do not trust in an economy, we trust in God, and even now, during these times, God is calling out to us all, return to me. The dollar bill says, "In God we Trust," however, people don't act like it. People act like,

'In the economy we trust.' People don't act like

'In God we trust.'

The word Rend in the Hebrew language in this passage means:

Oara: *Cut out. To Tear*

The word Heart in this passage means

Lebab: *To be enclosed as with fat. With love. Breast. Comfortably. Tender-heart. Mind. Understanding*

The word garments in the Hebrew means:

Begad & Bagad:_*Deal deceitfully, offend. Treacherous. Unfaithful. A covering. Clotihing. Apparel. Lap. Rag. Raiment. Robe. Vesture. Wardrobe*

God longs for us to cut off, to rip out of our life anything treacherous in our minds that is not pleasing to Him or is causing us harm. He longs for us to have a wardrobe inside that is pleasing to Him. It is not as important our outside clothing as it is our inside clothing. What is on the inside and underneath the skin is what God is most concerned about.

The word rend is an action and it requires us to cut out and rip out and tear out everything that is not pleasing to Him. The things that are not pleasing to Him in our lives hurt us and hurt the very plan that God has for us. He longs to prune us, and weed out anything that is keeping us from growing in Him and in His good will for our lives.

It is not as important to be concerned with the clothes we wear, as it is our relationship with God, our heart issue is what God is most concerned about. He cares for us, loves us, and does not want us to fear the economy. He wants us to cry out to him, from the deepest part of our being, and tell Him we are afraid, and He will help us. He will have pity on us. He is gracious and compassionate; slow to anger and abounding in love.

In American culture we are quick to get angry. We get angry especially when things don't go our way. We want short lines at the bank, short lines at the grocery store, short commercial breaks on TV, we want more green lights and fewer red lights. We want the traffic to speed up or we get mad. We are not a people that are slow to anger and I believe our love is growing cold.

However, God is not quick to get angry. He is slow to get angry and His love abounds so much for us. I met my real dad in the fall of 2002 for the first time in a prison cell in Georgia. I was in my thirties but when I met him, his love for me was abounding, over flowing; his long lost daughter had come to visit him in his cell, one he never thought he would see again. We had been separated from the time I was eight months old until then, and he sat day after day in a prison cell longing for me to visit. When I finally came, his love for me was abounding. Instead of being angry at me, his love was over flowing.

If an earthly father knows how to love his daughter, one who has been incarcerated for years, how much more does the One who created you love you? We must believe it and have faith, even if we are losing it all. He is in charge and wants His best for us.

So *even now*, no matter what state you are in, rend your heart, come back to the God who is slow to anger, and abounding in love for you. He desires for you to not be afraid, and to trust in Him, not the economy, and not the dollar bill.

Questions:

1. What is God's economy about?
2. What does God's economy look like?
3. Do you trust in your job, & the world's economy?

Quiet Time:

Take a dollar bill, say, a 1.00 bill, look at the words In God we Trust. Now picture that dollar bill being in God's economy, not the world's economy. Pretend you could not spend that dollar bill on anything. Decorate the dollar bill with what the Lord's system is. You could put angels on the dollar bill where the face of the president is. You can put bible verses on it. Whatever it is you want to do with that dollar bill, decorate it in light of what God's economy is. Put the dollar bill where you can be reminded that it is His economy, not the world's economy.

Now, take another dollar bill and give it to a ministry this week, or to a homeless person, or to someone in need. Just one dollar bill. Give it away. As you do, pray that God will help you have kingdom mentality in regards to the economy, and that you trust Him with your finances, and you are not afraid.

If possible, do not read a newspaper, or watch the news all week long. Take that time that you would read a newspaper, or watch the news to focus on the good things of your life.

Day 30

Fear of God not Revealing His Plan

Amos 3:7 & 4: 13 Surely the Sovereign Lord does nothing without revealing his plan to his servants the prophets. He who forms the mountains, creates the wind, and reveals his thoughts to man, he who turns dawn to darkness, and treads the high places of the earth-the Lord God Almighty is His name.

The word tread in Webster's dictionary means: To step or walk on or over, to walk or proceed along. To beat or press with feet. To copulate with-used of a male bird. To form To move or proceed on or as if on foot. To set foot has gone where others fear to tread to put ones foot

The Lord desires to reveal His plans to us. It is clear in the above scripture that the Lord loves to communicate directly with His children. He desires to reveal his thoughts, plans, and dreams for them to them. He has thoughts for you and He wants to reveal them to you. This can not happen if we are consumed with our fear. To be able to hear God, and listen to what He has for us, we must ask Him to help us let go of our fear, confess it, and repent from the fear itself.

God is treading for us also. He is walking over us, above us, and going to the ends of the earth for us. He is flying over us, as a bird flies, and God sees from above, not from within our circumstance. He does not see as we see. He sees as a loving Father, not a harsh dictator, or mean abusive father. Jesus went to the cross for us, and descended into hell for us. Jesus was laughed at, mocked, ridiculed, spit upon, and died for our sins. He went to the cross for us, even when He did not want to, yet He chose to go to the cross, and die for our sins. It is an amazing love. God has already treaded where we fear to tread. God has gone to the places that we fear to go. God has already lost everything for our sake, and has given us the best gift of all, His Son, Jesus, and eternity with Him. That is our final home. That is our final destination. We are heaven bound.

It is God's job to deal with and carry our fears, not ours. God is strong enough to handle our fears, and He does not want us to be afraid in our humanness. He is up above, looking down, flying over us, and forming our lives in a loving manner. He sees us losing it all, our sanity, and material possessions, and our own way, and He says, "Do not fear. I am fighting for you; I am going to the places that you do not want to go for you. I am there; I see what you are going through, but hold on, Help is coming. Just turn to me, return to me, fear not, for I am going to reveal to you my thoughts for your life."

Maybe you landed in a job just because you had to pay your bills. Maybe you ended up in an apartment because your boyfriend lived there. Maybe you ended up in a state because you thought it was pretty. Maybe you built the house you wanted to live in, but did not seek God before you built it. Maybe many of the decisions you have made in your life as a believer, you have done for status quo, or for a name for yourself, or because you are afraid of poverty.

Whatever the reasons you have based your decisions on up until this point, if you have not sought God before you made that choice then that could be part of the reason you are going through what you are going through. I made many decisions in my life without seeking God first, as a believer, and when I did, those plans failed.

I took jobs because I had to pay the bills. I moved to a state because my boyfriend lived there. The first time I did that I did not seek God, the second time I did that, I did seek God and we ended up married. I have made friends with people that I should not have. I have spent money on things I should not have and I have made bad choices without seeking God.

It is much more freeing when I say to God, "What do you want me to do in this situation or circumstance." Then when I listen quietly, He reveals His thoughts and plans for my life to me and when I obey, they succeed. They may not turn out the way I want, but they turn out for my best, His glory, and the way He wants.

Do not fear. Seek God in all your decisions and then you will know that He is mapping, planning, and treading the places of your life for you. In this time of uncertainty and turmoil within our economy, don't you think God knows? He knew who all the players were in the mortgage companies, banks, government, etc. and who made decisions without seeking Him, and who made decisions seeking Him. He knows this is happening. This same God, who knows what is going on with our economy, is the God who created the world.

For we read in Amos that God formed the mountains, creates the wind, and turns dawn to darkness! This is the God that desires to live in you and reveal His thoughts and plans for your life to you. It is not about the economy.

We have had many financial struggles in our marriage and we have made some mistakes. God is revealing His thoughts and plans to us and for our lives together, and I am letting go of my fear to Him daily. God is going to do great things in our marriage and through us for His glory as we continue to seek Him, the creator of the wind. God wants to create things in us and through us.

God wants to use you. The creator of the wind is creating something in your life that you can not see. That something that He is creating is so powerful and it is as powerful as the wind that blows. God wants to blow you away into the unknown territory and lead you to places that you have never been.

God has a purpose for you, and desires for you to be free from the fear of your financial failure. It's not about you or me. It's about the creator's purposes for our life.

The God who creates the wind can create something beautiful out of your life. Let Him begin to reveal His thoughts and dreams for you. Watch those plans succeed.

IF you are afraid of anything today, God wants you to let that fear go, because He is traveling with you wherever you go, and He treads the places of the earth that people are afraid of! God goes, where we don't want to go! God treads to those places that we are so afraid of treading. Don't fear, realize, trust, believe, and know for certain that God is treading with you, wherever you go, and you need not be afraid!

Questions:

1. Do you think God was surprised that the banks would collapse?
2. Do you think God was surprised that our economy would fall?
3. Do rising gas prices scare you?
4. Do you think God can give you a raise to suit the gas prices?
5. Are gas prices rising in God's economy?

Quiet Time:

If at all possible sometime this month, or next month make a plan to go hike a mountain somewhere. It could be a small mountain, but hike up one. When you get to the top, consider God and His formation of that mountain. Realize, reflect, and ponder on all the ways that God is and has carried you up the mountains of your life. Realize that He formed that mountain, He formed you, and He's got everything under control. Take a picture of you on top of that mountain. Frame it when you get home, and put the above verse inside or on that frame to remind yourself daily that the Lord formed the mountains and He treads on the places of the earth that people are fearful of.

If you can not get to a mountain, climb to the top of a tall building using the stairs, or something that is high. If you are afraid of heights, have someone go with you, and tell the Lord to go with you and to tread with you.

Day 31

Fear of not being God's Warrior

Obadiah 1: 9 & 12 & 15 Your warriors, O Teman will be terrified, and everyone in Esau's mountains will be cut down in the slaughter. You should not look down on your brother in the day of his misfortune, nor rejoice over the people of Judah in the day of their destruction, nor boast so much in the day of their trouble. The day of the Lord is near for all nations. As you have done, it will be done to you: your deeds will return upon your own head.

I magine a warrior being terrified. The above scripture says, "Your warriors *will be* terrified." This is because of the sin they had committed. The warriors of Teman had done evil to others and God was saying here that whatever you have done, it will be done to you.

There have been all kinds of warriors in our lifetime and in the life time before us. Warriors come in all shapes and sizes. Warriors are currently in Iraq fighting for us. There have been good and evil warriors. I have never, ever heard of anyone saying, "Your warriors will be terrified." Yet, God said that and we must consider our ways towards others, especially those He loves.

God commands us in the above passage to not look down on others in the day of their mis-fortune, nor rejoice when others are being destroyed, nor boast about anything.

Throughout history God has destroyed nations for their pride. He abhors pride. Pride comes before a fall, the Titanic sank because the builders of that ship were prideful saying it would never sink. Never say never is what I say.

I was a woman debt free just a little over a year ago and proud of that fact. I had traveled the world doing missions for the Lord, and remained out of debt. I had not a car payment or credit card debt of any kind. I did not believe that God wanted me to raise support for missions and be in debt. So in my twenties, I worked hard to get my vehicle paid off, and pay off my credit cards.

Just about one year ago was when I got into my credit card debt. It started innocently, putting schooling on the card and then it just kept going. I definitely have made some mistakes financially the past year. I believe my pride for being debt free could have been my down fall. If you have some pride today it is time to confess it and move on. Do not hold onto your pride for whatever reason because it could be your down-fall. Pride is a suttle thing and it sneaks up on you so ask God to show you if you have some pride.

Now, I am in debt and struggle with fear. Some of it is my fault. It's not all my fault, however, I have to ask God's forgiveness for where I have gone wrong financially, repent, and ask His help to give me His plans to get me out of debt.

I was a strong warrior of the Lord, a spiritual warrior in India, Mongolia and other nations of the world. The bible calls us warriors-that is not a prideful statement. In the New Testament we read all about the warrior within, and how God wants us to put on the full armor of God, and fight with the sword of the Spirit!

I became a warrior afraid because of my own sin, getting into financial debt, and becoming a slave to the lender. A fearful warrior is a defeated warrior. They can not fight for themselves anymore, they have lost the battle, it's over, done, finished. They are no longer a fighting, brave warrior. Instead they are afraid, defeated, alone and terrified. This is what being in debt has done to me. Yet God is delivering me from fear as I have gone through the bible and continue to seek Him in regards to fear.

Satan likes to play with that fear. Last month I was in Home Depot, and a customer service girl said, "Hey, your credit card is about to go up 24% and there is nothing you can do about it." Yesterday, my husband talked to the card services person on the phone, and she said that we could get our interest rate lowered. My husband got our Home Depot interest rate down to 4%.

This is what satan can do to a person who is already struggling with fear. Being unemployed right now, and my husband just opening up his consignment shop, we are struggling to pay the mortgage. When that lady said that, fear went up my spine. I chose not to whine about it and discuss this with my husband. He took care of it. Had I called everyone I knew and whined about the interest rate I would have been focusing on the problem and not a solution.

A true warrior in Christ does not whine. A true warrior in Christ prays and trusts Him with the outcome.

God wants us to be Warriors and not whiners. God wants us to be winners, and not whiners.

God does not want us looking down on others because of their financial difficult time. He wants us to help each other during our struggles of life. God wants us to be Warriors and fight with prayer and the Word of God. He does not want us whining about our problems. He does want us praying to Him with a wide open heart seeking His will for our lives, and thanking Him every step of the way for all the wonderful things He is doing in our lives during these days.

We can be Warriors for the Kingdom during this time and let go of our whining. We can then watch God do mighty things in us, through us, and for Him.

God wants you to be a beautiful bride with combat boots and He as the handsome groom with a sword of the spirit in your hand. God's prince or princess does not have to be afraid when the economy has fallen and it can't get up.

Put on your armor and fight like a warrior princess, (or prince). Be a warrior and not a whiner.

Questions:

1. Do you whine to others about your problems?
2. Are you in financial debt?
3. What would be your ideal outcome about a financial struggle you are facing? (example would be to get a credit card paid off, or have lower interest on it, or something like that)

Quiet Time:

Take your credit cards, and take your bills and put them in a pile. One by one pray over them, and ask God for deliverance from debt, and fear about paying your bills. Talk to the Lord about your financial struggles. Take out a sheet of paper, and write down all your credit card balances, and bills. Beside your credit card balances put paid off in big letters, and ask God to help you pay them off. Start with the smallest credit card, once that is paid off, take that monthly payment, add it to the next payment of the next credit card, and soon that one will be paid off. Do this until you are out of debt.

The next time someone starts whining to you about their problems, or you start whining about yours, catch yourself. One way to do this is by wearing a rubber band around your wrist, and each time you begin to hear yourself whine, or hear someone whine, pull the rubber band. Do this task for at-least 25 days to get yourself conditioned to not whine. Force yourself to become a prayer warrior, and to be a warrior about your problems, and others problems, and not a whiner. If you can think of anything else that will help you to go to God first with your problems instead of someone else, do it. Make steps this month to become a warrior. A warrior fights in the spirit, and combats the enemy. You could also go to the salvation army, or thrift store, and see if there are combat boots, and a sword that you can purchase for cheap. Also, find a doll or baby that whines. Purchase these items, and put them in your room. The next time you whine, push the button of the baby doll that whines, and you can hear how you sound to others and God when you whine about your problems. Put the combat boots and sword somewhere for you to see every single day to remind you that you are becoming a warrior princess. Put together anything for yourself that reminds you that you are a warrior princess, a fighter in the Kingdom of God and not a whiner.

Start making a list of solutions for your problems. As you focus on solutions, instead of the problem, you become more like a Warrior, instead of a whiner.

Get all dressed up, go stand on a rock somewhere, and get your picture taken. Frame that picture and write on it, 'I am standing on the promises of God.' To remind yourself that you stand on the word of God, and you will not fear.

Day 32

Fear of Drowning in your Sin

Jonah 2:1 & 6 In my distress I called to the Lord and he answered me. From the depths of the grave I called for help and you listened to my cry. To the roots of the mountains I sank down; the earth beneath barred me in forever. But you brought my life up from the pit, O Lord my God.

Once upon a time in a land far away a man named Jonah was called by God to go to a place called Nineveh. Jonah didn't want to go there because he didn't like the people of Ninevah! He ran and ran until he was swallowed whole and alive by a whale. Young Jonah was inside the belly of a whale-alive for three days!

Perhaps you have a stronghold in your life of fear. It is so strong that it engulfs you. The roots are as strong as the roots that hold down a 100 year old oak tree.

Perhaps you have gone from being a pauper to the palace and now you are down again. You have sunk down to the roots of the mountains and now they hold you there. You feel captive. No, you are not captivated by the strong mountains that surround you. You are captivated by the fear that you felt as you were falling down that mountain.

A stronghold in our life happens when we focus on that fear day after day after day when it begins to consume us. It takes root in the deepest part of our soul and refuses to let go. It is so strong that you may not know how to get those roots burned out of your soul.

Jonah was a man with a call on his life and at first, he ignored it and argued with God about it, and he ran away from that call. In the end, Jonah ended up in the ocean, in the belly of a whale for three days. While in that whale, Jonah went through fear, anxiety, and hopelessness.

The above scripture doesn't spell it out but Jonah was inside the belly of the whale. The scripture says that it felt like a grave-like death inside that dreadful place! After three days the fish begins to stink and Jonah says that he felt as though he had sunk to the lowest parts of his life.

If you are like Jonah, and have run away from the call of God on your life, it is time to call out to Him. Maybe you ran so far that a whale has swallowed you whole. Now you are choked out by the internal organs of the whale and can not seem to get out from whatever it is that has such a stronghold in your life.

Tell God you are sorry and in distress. Tell Him that the whale has got you so surrounded and entangled that you don't know how you can ever get out of the mess you are in.

You may be in the belly of the whale and the whale that has swallowed you are your bad decisions, the loss of your job, or a bad relationship that entangles you. It could be something deeper like drugs or alcohol. Any of these things can keep you from the will of God. Maybe you are in a mountain of debt and you believe you will never be free to do what God wants for you because you are swallowed up by debt.

Don't believe that lie. If God has called you to something then God has all power and authority to deliver you from the deepest part of the engulfing sea.

Maybe you feel so low in your life. You have no money, no job, no car, and have lost so much the last few years. You could feel low because you failed college or high-school or failed in a marriage. There are many things in life that can make us feel as though we have come to the lowest point of our lives.

Maybe you have sunk so low and feel so guilty that you just can't seem to get out from under that guilt. Maybe shame or remorse has you entangled. Maybe the things of this world and the cares of this world have sucked the life out of you and you have sunk down to the deepest part of the sea.

I don't know what you have gone through but your Creator does. The same God that knew that Jonah been swallowed alive and whole is the same God that sees you swallowed alive and whole by the worries of this world. God is the One _who can make you whole_! Call out to Him in your distress, in your lowest point and He will deliver you.

After Jonah cries out to the Lord Jonah is set free from the belly of the whale. Jonah ends up preaching the gospel to the very place where God had told him to go-Nineveh.

If you are in distress today, you have all authority in heaven to cry out to God and ask Him to remove that mountain of fear that is engulfing you, and He will do it. You must pray in the name of Jesus, who is your deliverer. God wants to deliver you from the belly of the whale, the stronghold of fear. He wants to cut off those roots of fear that are so embedded in your soul and it may be painful to let go.

Another way that the Lord gets rid of roots and strongholds of fear is burning them up inside of us. He refines us with fire,(the whale was Jonah's fire), so that we can become pure gold. He burns up the impurities of our lives, in our soul, by His power and might, to deliver us from the belly of the whale.

I remember several years ago I was at Youth with a Mission during a time of prayer and worship. God gave me a vision. I saw a picture of fire within my soul, and that fire beginning at my toes working it way up to my head. Inside of me I saw several roots, thick ones around my body, and the roots were burning up, slowly, but surely. God was dealing with me not about fear at that point in my life, but burning up a relationship that I had in my past that needed to be healed. That is how God healed me, by burning up the dead stuff, the strongholds of my soul.

This is what He wants to do in your life. Allow the God of Jonah free you from the mountain of fear that is so embedded in you. Allow the roots to be burned up. Allow the impurities of fear that have swallowed you whole to be burned away completely. God doesn't want you to be swallowed up by life's problems, sins or pains. He wants you set free to do His will.

Questions:

1. Is there a stronghold of fear, uncertainty, negativity, pride, anxiety or whatever in your life?
2. Is there something in your life that holds you back from doing all that you are supposed to be doing?
3. If so, what or who is it, and what can you do to get rid of it?

Quiet Time:

Write down whatever it is your strong hold is. If it is fear, write it on a sheet of paper in big black letters. If it is a bad relationship, write that down. If it is pride, write it down. Now take a match, or lighter and go outside some place safe. Light the thing on fire, and watch God burn up the strong hold that is in your life. As it burns up pray and ask the Lord to help you keep this out of your life.

Go get some seeds and a pot and plant your favorite flower in it and watch it grow. As it grows, and becomes complete write on the pot, "God has planted beautiful seeds in me" (If you already have a pot with your beautiful flower grown, then go get that pot and write it down with some permanent paint.

Day 33

Fear of God not Forgiving You

Micah 7: 18 & 19 Who is a God like you, who pardons sin and forgives the transgression of the remnant of his inheritance? You do not stay angry forever but delight to show mercy. You will again have compassion on us; you will tread our sins underfoot and hurl all our iniquities into the depths of the sea.

While Jonah was in the whale God was treading and longing to hurl Jonah's sin right out of Jonah's life! God wanted to free him from that whale. There is that word again, tread. Sometimes to get His point across God repeats Himself.

God did not want Jonah in the whale; He wanted Jonah's sin of disobedience in the deepest parts of the sea. God wanted Jonah's obedience, and if Jonah had obeyed, he may have never ended up in the whale in the first place. God was up above watching Jonah in that whale, realizing that Jonah would soon return to Him, and cry out to Him. God again, had compassion on Jonah and God will again have compassion on you.

He forgives our sins as far as the east is from the west. He throws them out to the sea and remembers them no more. Jonah in the whale is a picture of how God views sin. He hates sin. He hates our sin, and He wants it destroyed, down to the depths of the sea, engulfed in the whale, drowned out, in the darkness, and held down by the roots of the mountains. He does not want that fear to come up out of the depths of the sea and engulfing us. He wants us free to do His will, to obey Him, to do what He has called us to do! What a merciful, loving God we have.

The word hurl in Webster's means:

To throw with great force. To send with great vigor, to thrust. To throw down, to over throw. To utter vehemently. To vomit.

God is hilarious. God takes our sin, and thrusts it out, sends with great vigor, throws it down, over throws it, and vomits it out of our lives! Isn't that wonderful good news! We do not have to have any strongholds in our lives of fear or sin. We can allow the God who created us to vomit it out of our life, forever, to the deepest part of the sea! That is pretty deep in itself. That is powerful, profound, and hilarious. To think God may vomit? If that's not funny, I don't know what is.

I don't know about you, but when I studied the word hurl, it got me so excited, that I wanted God to vomit out every single sin that I had ever committed in my life to the depths of the sea. I wanted His healing power in my life so badly that I wanted Him to reveal sins to me so that I could confess them and get them out of my life, entirely, forever, gone, banished, and, well, vomited out forever!

If any of you have ever been sick, like I was sick in India, you know what I am talking of when you read the word vomit. When I was in India, I was sick so badly, that I thought I was literally going to die. I had no relief for several hours other than being sick. I had no clean water, no wash cloth, no chicken soup for the soul, or chicken broth, or orange juice. All I could do was just get sick and lie there and think about how wonderful death would be right then and there. Anything was better than being as sick as I was in India.

That is how it is with our sin. God hates our sin, and wants it gone. He wants it out of our lives forever because it keeps us bounded up, and rooted in all kinds of issues and problems. Sin makes us sick, and all those around us sick.

If we allow God to thrust our sin to the deepest part of the sea, and that begins by confessing it, whether it is fear, or any other sin, then we won't be sick anymore! He will take our sin, and get rid of it for us! It won't come back; it's a permanent thrust to the sea. Sin will only come back in our life if we allow the sin to come back. Fear only comes back when I focus on it, when I dwell on it.

I don't know about you, but I want to get sick. So sick of me and my sin that I never have fear again.

Questions:

1. What sin needs to be hurled out of your life?
2. What are some sins that you have done that are sickening to you?
3. What sin is in your life that you want God to be sick about, and vomit it out of your life?
4. What is something so ugly, so disgusting in your life, that you just can't have it anymore?
5. Are you in the belly of a whale?
6. What do you need to do to get out of that whale?
7. What have people done to you, or towards you that makes you sick?

Quiet Time:

Pray for those people, forgive them and ask God to help them get sick of themselves.

Now, your exercise is going to be odd. Let something get moldy or rotten in your refrigerator. Pull it out when it is, and smell it and get downright disgusted with it. Throw it out abruptly, and picture God throwing out your most disgusting sin, forever!

Day 34

Fear of God Not Caring about Your Troubles

Nahum 1:7 The Lord is good, a refuge in times of trouble. He cares for those who trust in him.

Who do you trust?

In today's society, trust is a word that we have seemed to let go. We have all been hurt, and some hurt badly, so much so, that trust is a foreign word, not an American word. To trust someone is challenging, and not easily attained. It's almost as if trust is earned. It is not an automatic response to someone we first meet. We don't trust the stranger on the street and sometimes we don't even trust members of our own family.

This thought of trusting God can be a challenge-especially when things are not going our way. We want something, we don't get it. We want the job, the someone, the something, and we don't get it, so we have a hard time trusting God when we don't get what we want. With job lay offs we are not now able to just go to the grocery store and buy what we want, we are all watching every penny. We are not traveling like we used to, and we are not just giving our money away. We are holding onto what we can save, salvage, and keep in our freezers for a rainy day.

What is trust?

Trust is a noun and a verb.

It means: *reliance on the integrity, strength, ability, surety of a person or thing; confidence. Confident expectation of something; hope. Confi-*

dence in the future payment for property or goods received. A person on which one relies. The condition of one to whom something has been entrusted. The obligation or responsibility imposed on a person in whom confidence or authority is placed; a position of trust. Charge, custody or care, to leave valuables in someone's care. Something committed or entrusted to one's care for use or safekeeping, as an office, duty, or the like; responsibility; charge.

Let's make up a sentence.

Our new definition of trusting in God:

To trust in God means to rely on the integrity, strength, ability, and surety of Him, knowing that I can have the expectation that He is going to take care of all the future payments of my mortgage, groceries, and bills, relying on Him alone, and in the condition I am in. I need Him to be responsible for me, to be my authority, and in charge of my life. I am safe in His arms. He cares for me.

Well, what do you think? Do you believe all that about God? Some days I do and some days I don't. The longer I live, the more I realize that I am able to completely trust Him for my well being, my all, my groceries, my utilities, my mortgage, my life. This has been a learning process for me. For some, this kind of trusting in God is easier than it has been for me. I don't know about you, but you can ask God if you really trust in Him, or if you trust in yourself.

If you were in a great financial need, through no fault of your own, would you trust Him? Can you let go of worrying about finances, realizing that God cares for you and you can rely on Him to pay your bills, or do you depend on your own strength, ability, and resources to finance your own life? If you got in an accident tomorrow, and you couldn't work, how long could you survive on what you have in your bank accounts?

We like to think we trust God. I definitely would have said five years ago, I trust God. I was on the mission field over seas, and all my finances came in for my trips and food that I needed. I did not worry about money. Now that I have been laid off suddenly from a $42,000 a year job, which was when I bought my house, I've been more concerned about money more than in my past. God will use things in our lives to test the condition of our heart. I know many Christians that say they trust God, but are they hoarding their finances, unwilling to take a less paying job because God may have a different plan for their life? They say that job won't afford to pay my bills.

What if God has a different plan?

I am there right now. I have an offer for a Teller job and I have accepted it. The pay is half of what I was making at the other bank.

Am I afraid of taking a pay cut? Sure, the fear thoughts have come my way. I had to really struggle with God about the job.

My husband is just starting out with his consignment shop and my job will cover the mortgage, but nothing else. Do I trust God that He is going to take care of my well being during these days? It's not that I don't have a husband that isn't willing to provide for me. He is an out of work builder and making a career change. He will do whatever it takes for this family. It is not my husband's job to provide for every single thing for my life, it is God's. I can trust in God that God is going to take care of this family in the midst of our financial crisis.

When the Israelites were in the wilderness for forty years they had manna every day. Manna was provided for them out of the sky and it was honey wafers. I believe whole-heartedly that this manna was from the body of God Himself and that God was feeding them from Himself! I believe the manna was pure and that is why God got so upset with them when they complained about the manna. They had no idea what God was feeding them. To them it looked like a honey wafer but to God it was pure bread from Him. It was enough to sustain them and God was saying to them that he would sustain them all their life.

The men couldn't work for provision for the family and there were no deer to shoot in the middle of the wilderness. Again, God sustained them every single day. It was not what they wanted but it was what they needed to sustain them.

God will take care of us. You may not be able to live in your dream house by the sea, or in a castle in the clouds, but your God, who is your refuge in times of trouble, will take care of you, if you trust in Him. He will care for you in the ways that is best for you and your family. God cares for those who trust in Him.

Do you trust Him?

Questions:

1. What do you trust in?
2. Who do you trust in?
3. Where do you put your trust?
4. Do you really trust God, even if you lost your job tomorrow?
5. Have you ever thought about that you may have really secretly thought, "I'm afraid I don't *really* trust God?"

Quiet Time:

Now, go to McDonald's and order your favorite beverage, whether it be a milk shake, coke or whatever. Sit at McDonald's for a while and watch all the people going in and out of there ordering their food. What do you see? What do you hear? Watch, look and listen. People are pretty sure that

McDonald's is there, caring for their hunger and thirst, right? How much more can you trust the Lord? This exercise is powerful, so please do it.

Write about what you learn at McDonald's and the issue of trust.

Now, write out how you can now trust God for your every need. Write God a love letter telling Him you trust Him, and that you trust Him to care for your needs. Thank Him for everything in your life.

Day 35

Fear of Not being Noticed by God

Habakkuk 3:1 & 2 A prayer of Habakkuk the prophet, on Shigionoth.

L ord, I have heard of your fame; I stand in awe of your deeds O Lord; renew them in our day, in our time make them known' in wrath remember mercy.

A long time ago, a man named Habakkuk was on Shigionoth, and in that far away land Habakkuk had heard of God's fame.

<u>The word Shigionoth in the Hebrew means:</u> *A moral mistake*

In Habakkuk's day people were in moral rebellion, worshiping all kinds of idols other than the God of Abraham, Isaac and Jacob. They were doing what they want, when they wanted, living for themselves, and doing all sorts of detestable things in the sight of God.

Our life is all about the fame of God, not ours. God wants to be famous in the life of us, and wants to be known, well-known through the world. That is His goal, to be well-known to the ends of the earth before He comes back to take His bride home to be with Him for eternity.

God wants you to know Him personally, to walk, talk, dream and live with Him. He desires to make Himself known to you, and for you to fall in love with Him. He desires for your heart to be made whole by His mercy, and love. God wants you to have a wonderful life, a life filled with wonderful renewal and peace.

Maybe you have made a moral mistake and you can't seem to get over it. Our moral mistakes don't mean as much to God as it does for you to get to know Him. You can talk to Him about your mistake and move on from that mistake.

To get to know God, you must seek Him with all of your heart. Not money, not things, and not another person. God must be first. To get to know God, you need to hang out with Him, reading His word, asking Him to speak to you the hidden treasures that He wants to show you as you read. That is what I do while I write. I pray and ask God to show me hidden treasures and give me wisdom from His heart. That is His goal, to become famous in your life, to be well-known in your life.

What if Demi Moore, Stevie Wonder, Jackson Browne, Steve Tyler, Willie Nelson, Nicole Kidman, Brad Pitt, Mary Tyler Moore, Andy Griffith, Aunt Bee, (ha) Carol Burnette, Jimmy Buffet, Colin Powell, Rush Limbaugh, Dr. Laura, Dr. Phil, Oprah or any other famous person wanted to hang out with you and get to know you, how would you respond? I am sure, depending on the person, you would be thrilled. You would do your hair, look your best, clip your toes, and get your house in order to hang out with a famous person, even if for only a day. You would give your all and be on your best behavior at all times around that famous person. Now, what if that famous person decided to treat you out to dinner? What if that famous person said you can order whatever you want. What if they said that you could ask them whatever question you want, and they would listen to you and answer you all night?

God wants His fame to be known in your life and to hang out with you for eternity! He owns much more than all the famous people I have previously mentioned and He wants to give it all to you. He wants to give all His riches of peace, joy, life, love, laughter, happiness, rest, patience, kindness, goodness, gentleness, and self-control. All this and more He wants to give you, but you have got to make a move. You have got to hang out with

Him for a while, and become His friend. You have to read His word and ask Him questions. He will reveal Himself to you.

God has wonderful, marvelous things He wants to do in your life, for you, and through you. He wants to do these things for His glory, honor, and fame. Will you start making a point to get to know Him?

Hark, someone famous is knocking at your door! _That door is your heart_. That famous One is Jesus.

Questions:

1. What one famous person would you love to have dinner with?
2. What questions would you ask them?
3. What would your ideal answers be to you from that famous person? (this is the time to dream.)
4. Where would you like to hang out with this person?
5. What would you wear?
6. Would you want their autograph?
7. What would you have them autograph?

Quiet Time:

Whatever it is that you would have them autograph, a picture, a book or whatever, I want you to find that thing in your house and put the above scripture on that and sign it, "Love, God, the famous man in your life."

Go somewhere special with a person you love and hang out with them for a day. Talk to them about them. Ask them questions, and ask them to dream about their life. When you come home from that special time with that special person (a friend, a spouse, a parent, a child) you need to sit some place quiet and think about all they said to you during the day. Think about what they shared, and how you listened. This is the kind of relationship God wants with you.

Find a magazine with your special famous person, or download it from the internet, and print it out, or cut it out. Put that picture somewhere you can see it, perhaps in your bible. Write on that picture, "I would love to meet this famous person one day." Why? For a reminder that God is much more famous than that person, and He wants to meet you one day and do more for you in your life than that famous person can!

Day 36

Fear of not Pleasing God

Zephaniah 3:17 The Lord your God is with you, He is mighty to save. He will take great delight in you, he will quiet you with his love, he will rejoice over you with singing.

*H*ave you been delighted lately? What does the word delight do within you? Does it make your leap a little for joy, or smile on the outside?

There are many foods with the word delight in them. We all want to be delighted, but little seems to be delighting us these days. The news definitely does not delight us. People at work are grumpy; your spouse isn't in the best of moods. The word delight seems to have left the building or rather, planet.

What is delightful to you, in your soul? If something were to delight you, what would that look like? When was the last time you thought of the word delight?

The word delight means:

A high degree of pleasure or enjoyment. Something that gives great pleasure. To give great pleasure, satisfaction, or enjoyment to, to please highly.

Ok, here we go with another new sentence that we made up. God takes a high degree of pleasure and enjoyment in you. You are someone that gives great pleasure to God. God is satisfied in you and you please Him highly.

How does that satisfy you? Doesn't it just elate you to know that you bring enjoyment, pleasure to God and that you please Him *highly.*

What if your husband, boss, mother, father, or someone you greatly admire like Martin Luther King or some other hero of yours said that you have pleased them highly.

Although you can not see God, these are words from centuries ago, written just for you. In your here and now, wherever you are reading this, from your place of hurt, fear, concern, worry, moral mistake, God is pleased with you. Whatever it is that is troubling you, God is speaking right to you from the deep parts of the earth and delivering a message to you where you are, no matter what, that you, dear one, have pleased Him highly.

You do not have to be afraid of whatever is going on in your life, with the God who is your refuge delights in you right now where you are. Take a moment and feel His love and His delight around you. Believe in His love for you and accept it, and believe that you have pleased Him.

You were made for God's pleasure. You were made for God's enjoyment. God wants to enjoy you. God wants to bring you pleasure, and you to bring Him pleasure.

In the movie Chariots of Fire, the runner had been challenged by a nun that he should go into the ministry. The runner replied, "When I run, I feel God's pleasure." How could a runner say when I run I feel God's pleasure? Well, a runner is focused on one thing, running. While the runner is running, the runner is not focused on anything else, not their trouble, not their fear, not their problems. They just run. They run fast, and they are focused. It brought that runner pleasure in his life, knowing that God had created Him to run, and when that runner ran, and ran with all his might, he was running for God. God had created that man with a gift of running and that man was fulfilling his mission. Through the blood, the sweat, and the run the runner was focused on God, and bringing God pleasure.

Whatever it is in your life, that when you do it you feel the pleasure of God then that is what you were born to do!

Questions:

1. What do you do, that when you do it, you feel God's pleasure (it can be more than one thing)?
2. What delights you?
3. What brings you joy?
4. What makes you happy?
5. What makes you feel loved?
6. What were you born to do?

Quiet Time:

Take one step this week towards what it is your were born to do

Start doing something everyday in your life that when you do it you feel God's pleasure.

Now, go to the grocery store and treat yourself if you can, and buy something that delights you. You can find many foods with the word delight in it, if you want to buy that as a reminder that God is delighted with you, and is pleased with you. Then, come back home and enjoy your treat, whether it is a chocolate covered cherry, a reeses peanut butter cup, an apple, or raspberry delight ice cream, just delight in your pleasure, and as you sip, chew, and swallow, swallow the fact that God is delighting in you, and is pleased with you.

Day 37

Fear of Your Own Heart

Haggai 2: 5 "This is what I covenanted with you when you came out of Egypt. And my Spirit remains among you. Do not fear."

*H*aggai was a prophet and he and the Jews were building the temple after the Jews had returned from captivity. It was taking them 15 years to build the temple, and in the book of Haggai we read that they were more concerned about building their own homes rather than the temple of the Lord.

In a way we can't blame them for they had been in captivity for so long they so desired a place to call home. So they would focus on building their homes rather than the temple of the Lord. In those days that is where the Lord dwelled since Jesus had not yet come. The Lord could not dwell inside of men because men were defiled. Therefore a pure temple had to be built for the Lord to dwell. The temple would be considered a place of peace.

God had a covenant with the people since the time they came up from out of Egypt. The Israelites had been slaves in Egypt for hundreds of years crying out for a deliverer and Moses became their deliverer. Then they came into the Promised Land and began doing their own thing and God punished them for their disobedience, as a loving father disciplines their children for misbehaving.

Yet our God is a promise keeping covenant God. As in a marriage when two become married and they make a covenant to stick it out through thick and through thin. Marriages fail today miserably because people don't take the covenant seriously, but God does. Covenants are very serious to Him and He keeps every single covenant and promise He has ever made. The Israelites would be blessed in the end, yet through the book of Haggai we read how during the building process God is providing for them or not providing for them. He sends them fruit and seed to plant and grow and He provides everything they need for the foundation and the building process.

Yet during the process they forget this and don't remember the Lord their God. God dries up the land, makes the lumber moldy, and reminds them that He is their provider. They are not their provider, although they like to think they are. It is God who is caring for them during the whole entire process and all He requires is for them to return to Him and remember the Lord their God and to not fear because He loves them and is going to give them a wonderful life.

<u>The word covenanted in the Hebrew means:</u>

Karath: *To cut. To destroy. To consume. To make an alliance with. To bargain by cutting flesh and passing through the pieces. To be chewed. To fail. To be freed. To hew down. To make a league. To lose to perish.*

This word covenanted means something different than the word covenant. Covenant and covenanted have different meanings in the Hebrew language. It is a beautiful thing that God wants to remove the fleshly stuff out of our life, the rotten mud and dirt of our life to make us whole. He longs to destroy and cut our sinful flesh and pass through the dirty pieces of it to make us pure. He longs to remove all impurities of our life, and He will pass through the pig slop mess of our flesh and heal us. He will pass through us and cleanse us from all our dirt.

He longs to make alliance with us. An alliance is something permanent that can not be easily broken. He will not make an alliance with us and then become like an evil spy and betray us.

He will remain faithful to the end of that alliance. Usually, we are the ones who become like a spy and betray Him.

Jesus longs to pass through us, and reside in us permanently. He longs to fill up every fiber of our being with His purity. You may feel like you are completely living down in the garbage dumps of sin, depression, sadness, and despair. You may feel there is no way out of this mud pit, these dirty dumps that have begun to consume you. There is a way out of the dumps. You do not have to live in the dumps any longer. Jesus longs to chew up everything in your life that has messed you up.

The temple of the Lord is our heart and it is God who dwells there if we have asked Jesus Christ His Son to dwell there and ask Him to forgive us. Purity and impurity can not live together. Dirt and cleanliness can not live together. Garbage and trash can not dwell in you any longer if you completely give your life over to God. As a child of God you have no right living down in the dumps. You do not need to be a mud wrestler anymore. Mud wrestling is not attractive in the Kingdom of God. There is no place for you to wallow around in the mud if you are His precious blood bought child!

God will grant us fruit bearing tree to bear fruit all the days of our lives if we do this and abide and remain in Him. He desires to grant us peace in the temple as it says in Haggai 2:9.

He wants your house, your heart, to be free from weeds and mud! Get out of the mud-wrestling match with the demons of your sinful life. Allow the Son, Jesus Christ to wash you clean.

He wants the vine, the fig tree, and the pomegranate, oil, and new wine of your heart to grow and overflow in your life into the lives of others. He wants a solid foundation for your life to be laid inside your heart and for you to continuously remember the Lord your God and how He is delivering you from your fear and reminding you that He keeps His promises to you, loves you, and wants you to grow. All you must do is pray to Him and seek

Him. Ask Him to help you believe that He has a great plan for the fruit of your heart, His home, to grow for His purpose, honor, and glory. He will change you from the inside out to become a beautiful home for Him.

What does your heart look like today? What does God's building, home, look like? Is it dusty, moldy, and not a home that you would even want to live in, never mind God? Is your heart defiled as it talks about in the book of Haggai or is it a fruit bearing heart where pomegranates can grow peacefully, beautifully, and become delicious in your life? Is there seed left in the barn?

God says to consider carefully your ways in the building process. As you are beginning to allow God to re-build your heart His home remember that until then the pomegranates of your life were not growing tastefully but rather they were bitter inside your heart. As you draw close to God your bitterness and fear will disappear. People all around you will notice the beautiful ripe fruit tree you have become, all with the help of a loving covenant keeping God.

Questions:

1. What seeds need to be planted in your heart?
2. How can you water those seeds?
3. What comes out of you? (yelling, nagging, screaming-or love, joy and peace?
4. How do you talk to others?
5. How do you talk to yourself?
6. How do you treat yourself?
7. How do you treat others?
8. What is your favorite fruit?
9. If you were a fruit, what would you be, and why?

Quiet Time:

Go to the store and buy some of your favorite fruit and eat.

Go get some seeds, and whatever it is you need in your life, write on the seeds, 'kindness, joy, peace, happiness' and put them in your window.'

Plant a seed of kindness in someone else's life today, for you reap what you sow.

Day 38

Fear of the Soiled Stain in your Soul

Zechariah 3:4 & 8:19 The angel said to those who were standing before him. "Take off his filthy clothes." Then he said to Joshua, "See, I have taken away your sin, and I will put rich garments on you." This is what the Lord says: "The fasts of the fourth, fifth, seventh and tenth months will become joyful and glad occasions and happy festivals for Judah. Therefore love truth and peace.

The opposite of fear is peace and we can not have the peace of God in our life if we have fear. They don't communicate well together because they are opposite's and not in agreement with one another. One is scary -the other is lovely. One is harsh- the other is kind. One is dark- the other is light. Fear and peace are in opposition to each other continuously. It is a battle for our souls! Our hearts are God's home and our eternal home with Him is in heaven.

Fear and peace can not dwell together in harmony and God wants all fear banished from our life. Fear is filthy clothing wrapped around our minds and hearts and it is disgusting in God's sight. Fear is sin. Fear keeps our heart entangled, ensnared, and unable to hear the peace of God. The bible says that God's sheep hear His voice and if the voice you are hearing inside is fear you are not hearing His voice. His voice is a voice of peace.

To love truth and peace is to hate fear. To love truth and peace is a commandment from God. It requires action on our part. It is a choice to love, a choice to banish fear, and a choice to get rid of fear from our life. We can not do that without God's help for we read in the scripture above that God takes away our sin. He removes the filth from our hearts that hinder us from a deeper walk with Him.

<u>The word filthy in the above scripture in the Hebrew means:</u>

Tso: *Soiled*

<u>The word rich in Hebrew means:</u>

Ashar & Asar: To accumulate. To grow rich. *Sixscore Thousand.*

Now I am no bible scholar. I have used the Strong's Concordance to look up all words in this book. Whatever six score thousands means is what I want.

What about you? Doesn't Six score Thousand sound like a lot of wealth to you? God wants our soiled sin so much out of our life so that we can grow and become wealthy Kings and Queens for His Kingdom. The wealth may not be money, but it may be money. The wealth could be that you have so much peace in your life, a six score thousand amount of peace that nothing moves or shakes you. You could have so much joy, love and goodness in your life that people from all over want to come and hang out with you. You may gain a six score thousand of friends in your life because of the overflow of kindness that overflows out of you onto others.

Allow God to remove the soiled stain of sin in your life so that you can receive a six score thousand of whatever it is He wants to give you!

To love truth and peace almost goes against the core within us. Love and peace are words that our culture has lost. To love means to be patient, kind, gentle, to have self-control and much more. To love means that we have to develop love inside us. A seed of love has to be planted within us for us to be able to love correctly. God wants to plant that seed of love within our heart so that we can love truth love peace and hate what it is that keeps us from a wonderful life.

The filth of fear needs to go. Seeds of love and peace need to be planted so you can have truth and peace forever.

Whatever is going on in your life God desires for you to have a six score thousand of peace and to fear not!

Questions:
1. What is filthy to you?
2. What is filthy in your life?
3. What needs to be cleaned up in your life?
4. How can you develop more love in your life?
5. Have you lied lately?
6. Have you been hurt in your past by lies?

<u>Quiet Time:</u>

Ask God to remove all lies from your life

Ask God to plant a seed of love inside of your heart and ask Him to water it. To water love you can read the word of God daily and ask Him to take you on a love journey. Take the journey to love and truth and peace and all fear will be gone from you life. The dirt the filthy and the stains of fear that are inside you will be removed and you will find the riches of truth and peace growing inside you more every single day. What if you knew beyond a shadow of a doubt that you could have truth and peace inside you coming out of you for all around you to enjoy? Would you be more joyful? Wouldn't it be great to believe that you could have truth and peace no matter what circumstance, situation or unfortunate lay-off has occurred in your life? Your truth and peace should not come because someone likes you or not, you have money, a great job, a great place to live, or what-ever it is that you think brings you peace. Your truth and peace in your life comes from the love inside you that is planted by a tiny seed and grows over time.

Day 39

Fear of No Return

Malachai 3:6 "I the Lord do not change. So you, O descendants of Jacob, are not destroyed. Ever since the time of your forefathers you have turned away from my decrees and have not kept them. Return to me, and I will return to you," says the Lord Almighty.

Return to me are the most romantic words. Can you picture a good looking man or woman whom you love saying that to you? One you thought wanted nothing to do with you ever again because you had lied, cheated or done something so terrible to them? We have all been in a relationship like that. We have sinned against someone and just knew the relationship was over and we did not want it to be finished.

The word Return in the Hebrew means:

Shuwb: *Return to the starting point. To retreat. Break. Build. Circumcise. Dig. Do anything. Feed. Lay down. Lie down. Lodge. Make. Rejoice. Send. Weep. Answer. Averse. Bring back home again. Carry again. Come again. Convert. Deliver. Draw back. Fetch home again. Fro. Get back again. Give again. Go again. Go out. Pay. Pull in again. Put up again. Recall. Recover. Recompense. Rescue. Restore. Retrieve. Slide back. Still. Take back off.*

If you do not know how to get back to God because of some sin issue, just go back to the beginning. Start over again. Weep and cry on His shoulder and He will answer you. Allow Him to carry you back to His loving, strong, arms. Allow Him to rescue you and restore you back to Himself. It is not about you or your sin.

He is able to carry you back to the place where you belong and that is Home with Him.

Our relationship with God is much deeper than our earthly relationships. Our walk with God is something that will go into eternity forever. Our relationships on earth die when we die. Yet our relationship with God is for eternity and all we have to do is return to Him. We need to humble ourselves, tell Him we are sorry, ask for forgiveness and return to Him with the fullness of our hearts mind and soul.

It is not about us, what we have done, or false religion. God is in the business of healing our lives, and He continuously cries out from His very own heart, please, I beg you, return to me.

The Lord says,

"Come back to me my beautiful princess, my handsome prince. It does not matter what you have done I forgive you. Please return to me and watch what it is that I can do in your life and all that I have for you. I have so much to share with you to teach you to give and I can not without you in my life. I love you and that love does not change and is not based on the fact that you are not perfect. No one but me is perfect and so I have come to live in you and therefore that makes you pure in my sight. I forgive you, I am not angry at you. I accept your apology, and sincerity of heart. Thank you for coming back to me.

Thank you for returning to me. I have missed you. Let us walk through life together as one. Let us make a covenant and walk through the journey of life together and I will lead you. You only need to follow and I will lead you to beautiful places that you have never experienced. Take my hand and come with me. Return to me, my love."

Questions:

1. Have you run away from God?
2. Have you missed God lately?
3. Have you stepped outside of God's will?
4. Do you believe that God has changed?
5. Have you changed since the last time you and God were close?
6. Do you think God misses you?

Quiet Time:

Every journey begins with a single step, so it has been said. I will say every voyage begins with a small amount of faith.

Take one small step this week to return to the Lord, with your whole heart. It could mean that you read the word, or pray. It could mean that you fast, or it could mean that you give up a night of watching your favorite TV programs, to write and journal about God and what He is doing in your life. It could mean to take a nature walk in a beautiful park and focus on the beautiful trees, and think about all that God has made. Take one small step to return to God, you know what He is saying to you right now.

Write a love letter to *yourself* from the Lord, or copy the love letter that I have created for you in the beginning of this book and frame it.

Write a love letter to God from you.

Epilogue:

This concludes our journey from fearful fallacy, (wrong thinking) to the fearless fortress, (God the mighty deliverer.)

It is my prayer that you have made some significant steps in your life to become closer to the Fearless Fortress, the One who is able to build a strong life for you that will honor and glorify Him. You do not have to fear the economy or anything else. Just lean on the Fearless Fortress and allow Him to deliver you from all fear.

Prayer:

Lord Jesus, I come before you today and pray for every single person who has read this book. I pray Lord that you will be their Fearless Fortress and deliver them from any wrong thought. Help each person to be set free from all fear. May each person be free from all condemnation for that is not from You. I pray Lord that you will set people free all over the world from the fear that entangles us and keeps us from your will. If anyone had any reason to fear it was Jesus-yet He endured the cross, scorning its shame, for the joy set before Him. I thank you for every reader and I pray your joy over their life, your peace that passes all human understanding, your comfort where they need comfort, your healing where they need healing. Lead them Lord Jesus to do your will, your plan, and your purpose. Help them to be free from fear so they are able to do your will fearlessly for your Kingdom come. Free them from everything in their heavy heart. Amen~

God's Letter to you, His child

Written & Created By the author

Inspired by the Word of God

<u>Dear</u>_____ *(put your name in the blank!)*

<u>*Why are you running away from me, where are you going, and where*</u>
<u>*have you come from? (Genesis 7:*</u>
<u>*I am the God who sees you, in the deepest, darkest, desert places of your*</u>
<u>*soul (Genesis 16:*</u>
(Genesis 21:17-19)
What's the matter my child, don't be afraid. God has heard your crying
as you lie there and I have a well of water for you
And little by little I am driving things out of your life, so that you can
become fruitful enough to take possession of the land (Exodus 23:30)
Remember my child, I will grant peace in your land, and you will lie
down and no one will make you afraid (Leviticus 26:6)
The Lord desires to bless you, and keep you, and make His face shine
upon you. It is His will to be gracious to you, and give you peace
(Numbers 6:24-26)
And while you are in the desert, God is carrying you, as a Father car-
ries His son, all the way until you reach your planned out destination
(Deuteronomy 1:31)
Be strong and courageous, please don't be terrified, and do not be dis-
couraged for your God will be with you wherever you go (Joshua 1:9)
Remember, when you cry to the Lord, He will raise up a deliverer for
you, and you will have peace (Judges 3:9-11)
And now, my child, do not be afraid, I will do for you what you have
asked (Ruth 3:11)
Go in peace and may the God of Israel grant you what you have asked
(1 Samuel 2:17)

I have been with you, wherever you have gone and I have cut off all your enemies from before you. Now I will make your name great, like the names of the greatest men on earth and I will provide a place for you and plant you so you can have a home of your own and no longer be disturbed (2 Samuel 7:9-11)

For God rules over you, and wants to plant you under your own, restful, safe fig tree (1 Kings 4:24 & 25)

God has heard your prayers, seen your tears, and will heal you (2 Kings 20:5)

You will find rich good pasture, and your land will be peaceful, and quiet (1 Chronicles 4:20)

God loves you (2 Chronicles 2:11)

And so don't be afraid. Remember your God who is great and awesome (Nehemiah 4:14)

Life's golden scepter is out for you, you can boldly approach the throne. I think you are beautiful. (Esther 5:2)

Don't be disturbed, the King will grant you whatever you petition Him and desire. (Esther 8:6)

The Lord will make you prosperous again, and will give you twice as much as you had before, remember to pray for others (Job 42:10)

I desire to do wonders in your life, and I do have plans for you (Psalm 40:5)

Remember to trust Me, and lean not on your own understanding (Proverbs 3:5&6)

Banish anxiety from your heart, and cast off the troubles from your body (Ecclesiastes 11:10)

I desire to make a table of wonderful food for you, and give you a banquet, because I love you (Song of Solomon 2:4)

I long to give you the best of the land (Isaiah 1:19)

And to be gracious to you and show you compassion (Isaiah 30:18)

Before you were in the womb, I knew you, (Jeremiah 1:5)

I have heard your plea, and am near to you who when you call. Do not fear! (Lamentations 3:55-57)

Remember, don't be afraid (Ezekiel 2:6)

I am the Living God, and I endure forever, my kingdom will not be destroyed. I rescue, and I save, and I perform signs and wonders in heaven and on earth (Daniel 6:26)

Therefore, I will allure you, and will lead you into the desert to speak tenderly to you (Hosea 2:14)

So, even now return to me with all your heart. I am not concerned with your outer clothing, but more concerned with your heart. Be not afraid, and be glad, and rejoice. I am doing great things in your life, and am sending you grain, new wine, and new oil, enough to satisfy you fully. (Joel 2:12-14 & 21))

Remember child, I do nothing without revealing my plan to you (Amos 3:7)

If you cry out to me in your distress, I will rescue from the grace, the belly of the whale, and will listen to your cry. (Jonah 2:1)

I don't stay angry with you forever, I delight to show you mercy (Micah 7:18)

I am good and a refuge for you in a mess of trouble. I care for you, trust me. (Nahum 1:7)

I desire for my fame to be spread though the land, your life is about me, not you (Habakkuk 3:1)

I am mighty to save you, and I take great delight in you, I want to quiet you with my love, and I rejoice over you with singing (Zephaniah 3:17)

Remember, do not fear, I am the same God who brought the Israelites up out of Egypt (Haggai 2:5)

I desire for you to love truth and peace (Zechariah 8:19)

I do not change, I want you to return to me, and I will return to you (Malachi 3:6)

Love, Dad (Jehovah Jireh your Provider)

God has given Laura Irby a ministry that currently being developed-

Free to Fly Ministries. This ministry will inspire and motivate others to be free from fear.

Stay tuned for the second book in this series. Scriptures from the New Testament, the book is also called _Help Lord I'm Afraid-a voyage through the New Testament-_ to see what God says in the New Testament about fear.... coming soon in 2010.

Stay tuned also for the _Help Lord I'm Afraid Journal to be released after Christmas 2009_

Laura is available to come speak at your church or group.

You can reach the writer at Laura@freetafly.com

LaVergne, TN USA
17 March 2010
176319LV00004B/22/P